Continu Delivery and Site Reliability Engineering (SRE) Handbook

Non-Programmer's Guide

(DevOps, Microservices, Kubernetes & SRE manuscripts)

CONTINUOUS
DELIVERY AND
SITE RELIABILITY
ENGINEERING
(SRE)
HANDBOOK
Non Programmer's Guide

STEPHEN FLEMING

Topic 1: DevOps Handbook

Topic 2: Microservices Architecture Handbook

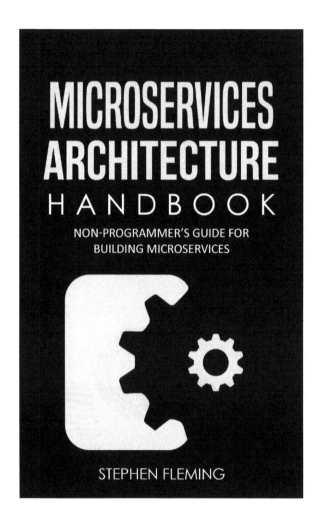

Topic 3: Kubernetes Handbook

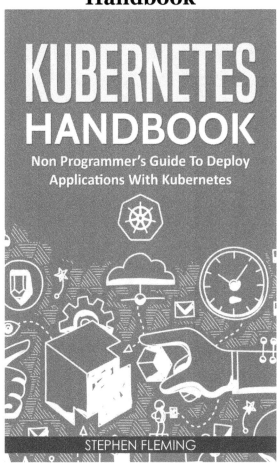

KUBERNETES
HANDBOOK
Non Programmer's Guide To Deploy
Applications With Kubernetes

STEPHEN FLEMING

Topic 4: SRE Handbook

This document is geared towards providing exact and reliable information in regards to the topic and issue covered. The publication is sold with the idea that the publisher is not required to render accounting, officially permitted, or otherwise, qualified services. If advice is necessary, legal or professional, a practiced individual in the profession should be ordered.

- From a Declaration of Principles which was accepted and approved equally by a Committee of the American Bar Association and a Committee of Publishers and Associations. In no way is it legal to reproduce, duplicate, or transmit any part of this document in either electronic means or in printed format. Recording of this publication is strictly prohibited and any storage of this document is not allowed unless with written permission from the publisher. All rights reserved.

The information provided herein is stated to be truthful and consistent, in that any liability, in terms of inattention or otherwise, by any usage or abuse of any policies, processes, or directions contained within is the solitary and utter responsibility of the recipient reader. Under no circumstances will any legal responsibility or blame be held against the publisher for any reparation, damages, or monetary loss due to the information herein, either directly or indirectly.

Respective authors own all copyrights not held by the publisher. The information herein is offered for informational purposes solely, and is universal as so. The presentation of the information is without contract or any type of guarantee assurance. The trademarks that are used are without any consent, and the publication of the trademark is without permission or backing by the trademark owner.

All trademarks and brands within this book are for clarifying purposes only and are the owned by the owners themselves, not affiliated with this document.

Table of Contents

MICROSERVICES ARCHITECTURE

KUBERNETES

SITE RELIABILITY ENGINEERING

Book 1- DevOps Handbook

Introduction to DevOps and its impact on Business Ecosystem

BONUS DEVOPS BOOKLET

Dear Friend,

I am privileged to have you onboard. You have shown faith in me and I would like to reciprocate it by offering the maximum value with an amazing gift. I have been researching on the topic and have an excellent "DevOps Booklet" for you to take your own expedition on DevOps to next level.

- Do you want to know the job requirement of DevOps Engineer?
- Do you want to know statistics of DevOps job available and mean salary offered?
- What are the latest trends in DevOps methodology
- People to follow on the latest on DevOps development

Also, do you want once in a while updates on interesting implementation of latest Technology; especially those impacting lives of common people?

"Get Instant Access to Free Booklet and Future Updates"

- Link: http://eepurl.com/dge23r

- QR Code : You can download a QR code reader app on your mobile and open the link by scanning below:

1. Introduction

DevOps is the buzzword these days in both software and business circles. Why? Because it has revolutionized the way modern businesses do business and, in the process, achieved milestones that weren't possible before. And in this book, you'll learn what DevOps is, how it evolved, how your business can benefit from implementing it, and success stories of some of the world's biggest and most popular companies that have embraced DevOps as part of their business. It is my hope that by the time you're done reading this book, you'll have a good idea of how DevOps can help your business grow.

So if you're ready, turn the page and let's begin.

2. What is DevOps

DevOps – or development and operations – is a term used in enterprise software development that refers to a kind of agile relationship between information technologies (IT) operations and development. The primary objective of DevOps is to optimize this relationship through fostering better collaboration and communication between development and IT operations. In particular, it seeks to integrate and activate important modifications into an enterprise's production processes as well as to strictly monitor problems and issues as they occur so these can be addressed as soon as possible without having to disrupt other aspects of the enterprise's operations. By doing so, DevOps can help enterprises register faster turnaround times, increase frequency of deployment of crucial new software or programs, achieve faster average recovery times, increase success rate for newly released programs, and minimize the lead time needed in between modifications or fixes to programs.

DevOps is crucial for the success of any enterprise because, by nature, enterprises need to segregate business units as individually operating entities for a more efficient system of operations. However, part of such segregation is the tendency to tightly control and guard access to information, processes and management. And this can be a challenge, particularly for the IT operations unit that needs access to key information from all business units in order to provide the best IT service possible for the whole enterprise. Simply put, part of the challenge in segregating business units into individually operating ones that are independent of each other is the relatively slow flow of information to and from such units because of bureaucracy.

Moving towards an organizational culture based on DevOps – one where the enterprise's operations units and IT developers are considered as "partners" instead of unrelated units – is an effective way to break down the barriers between them. This is because an enterprise whose culture is based on DevOps is one that can help IT personnel provide organization with the best possible software with the least risk for glitches, hitches, or problems. Therefore, a DevOps-based organizational culture is one that can foster an environment where segregated business units can remain independent but, at the same time, work very well with others in order to optimize the organization's efficiency and productivity.

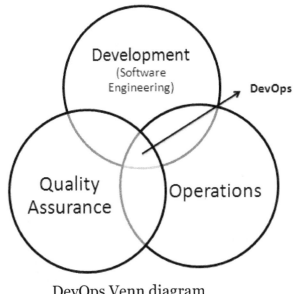

DevOps Venn diagram

Key Principles

One characteristic of DevOps is that it isn't grounded or dependent on stringent processes and methodologies. It's based more on key principles that allow an enterprise's key business units to efficiently work together and, in the process by breaking down any "walls" that may prevent optimal working relationships among such units. These key principles that guide an enterprise's DevOps are culture, measurement, automation and sharing.

Challenges Solved By DevOps

Just before the development of DevOps, it took several teams to collate the necessary data and informational requirements as well as writing code. After that, another team – a QA team – performed tests on new codes in a separate software development environment once the necessary requirements were met. Eventually, it's the same QA team that releases the new code for deployment by the enterprise's operations group. After that, the deployment teams are divided further into groups referred to as "silos" which include database and networking. And if you consider all the teams involved with the development and deployment of just one code, you won't be surprised why many enterprises suffer from project bottlenecks.

With such a set up, several undesirable things happen. One is that developers often become unaware of roadblocks for Operations and Quality Assurance that may keep the new programs from working as they were designed to work. Another thing that may happen is that as the QA and Operations teams work on so many features of the program, they may not have a true understanding of the purpose and value of the programs that are being developed/tested, which may keep such teams from effectively doing their work on such programs. Lastly, inefficiency and unnecessary backlogs are highly probable given each team or group has their own goals and objectives to achieve, which often times oppose those of the other groups, as well as the tendency to absolve themselves of responsibility for things that go wrong.

With DevOps, these potential problems can be addressed via creation of cross-functional teams that collaborate and share a common responsibility for maintaining the systems that are responsible for running software and other programs, as well as for prepping up the software so that they run on said systems with excellent feedback mechanisms for possible automation issues.

A Typical Scenario That Illustrates the Need for DevOps

Imagine that an enterprise's development team (the Dev team) releases a new program "over the wall" to Quality Assurance – the QA team. At this point, the QA team assumes the responsibility of discovering as many errors as possible in the new program, if any. Without any good working relationship – or any relationship at all for that matter – chances are high that the Dev team will be very defensive about the errors found by the QA team on their newly developed program, especially if there are lots of them. At which point, it's highly possible for the

Dev team to even blame the QA team for such errors or bugs in the program. Of course, the QA team will deny that it's them or their testing environment that's to blame for the errors or bugs and that at the end of the day they're just there to discover bugs that exist within the programs developers create. In other words, the QA team will just revert the blame for the errors back to the Dev team. It can become nasty.

Let's say, after several attempts, the bugs and errors were fixed and the program has fully satisfied the QA team. They now release the program to the operations team concerned, a.k.a., the Ops team. But the Ops team refuses to fully implement the new program because they feel that too much change too soon will hamper their ability to do their jobs effectively. So they limit their system's changes. As a result, their operating system crashes and blames the Dev team for it, notwithstanding the fact that their refusal to implement the system fully led to the crash.

Defending their honor and glory, the Dev team blames the Ops team for not using the program the way it is designed to be used. The blaming continues on for a while until finally, someone has the sense to intervene and eventually lead the teams to cooperate their way into fixing the program. But the delay and the losses were already incurred.

The Continuum

One very practical way to look at the various DevOps aspects is to use what's called the **DevOps continuum**. The vertical axis represents the 3 delivery chain levels of DevOps, which are continuous integration (lowest level), continuous delivery, and continuous deployment (highest level). The bottom horizontal plane or axis represents people's perceptions of what DevOps is focused on, where the left side represents an automation or tools perspective while the right side represents a culture perspective. Others feel strongly that DevOps must be focused more on culture than tools while for others, it's the other way around.

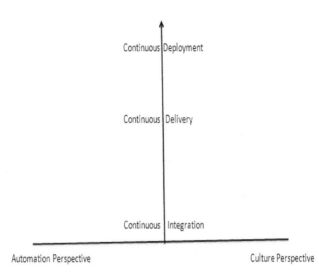

DevOps Continuum

The ideal location is the upper right hand corner, i.e., continuous deployment under a cultural perspective. Organizations that are located at this part of the continuum are considered as endangered species or unicorns simply because they're few and far in between. **Very good examples**

of these "unicorns" include Etsy, Netflix, Flicker, Amazon, Google and Pinterest.

Bloggers, coaches and some thought leaders usually paint a DevOps picture that's located on the upper right corner of the continuum. They may also have a strong bias towards either tools or culture. While it's not necessarily bad to have robust debates or discussions as to which is more important (tools or culture), the fact remains that organizations need both in order to optimize their productivity. Culture won't be productive without the necessary tools and tools won't work properly without the support of a very good culture.

It's important for organization to realize that moving up to the DevOps Nirvana spot in the continuum takes time. Many times, the first move is to combine tools, culture and continuous integration, which is at the lower wrung of the continuum. It shouldn't be an issue because DevOps isn't a very simple and easy activity and as such, it takes many baby steps and some time to maximize.

An optimal DevOps may be different for each organization because it's a blend of tools, culture, and maturity, all of which should make sense. And those that make sense is often relative and can change over time. What's crucial here is are continuous efforts to minimize – or even eliminate – any obstacles or bottlenecks for each software delivery phase through improvements in the automation processes and collaboration between silos or business units.

DevOps Maturity Phases

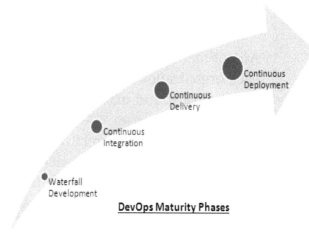

Continuous Deployment

Continuous Delivery

Continuous Integration

Waterfall Development

DevOps Maturity Phases

In order to keep track of an organization's DevOps progress, it's important to be cognizant of the maturity phases involved in DevOps. These include:

Waterfall Development: Prior to continuous integration, development teams write a ton of code for several months. When they're done with writing code, the teams will then combine their finished codes together so that they can release it. The code will come with different iterations or versions that are so different from each other and would probably undergo quite a number of changes that its integration process may take several months to complete. As such, this process may be considered as an unproductive one.

Continuous Integration: This refers to the quick integration of newly developed code with the existing main code body that will be released. This phase can help the team save a ton of time, especially when they're ready to release the code already.

This phase or process wasn't conceptualized by DevOps. Continuous integration is a practice that originated from the Extreme Programming methodology, which is an integral part of an engineering process called Agile. While it's been around for quite a while, this process or term was adopted by DevOps because every successful execution of continuous integration requires automation. As you learned in the DevOps continuum, continuous integration is the first level of the

DevOps maturity phase. This involves checking codes in, collecting it into a binary executable code in most cases, and doing basic testing to validate the code.

Continuous Delivery: This phase may be considered as an extension of the previous one and is stage 2 of the DevOps stage. During execution of this DevOps phase, adding extra automation and testing is needed in order to make newly developed codes ready for immediate deployment with practically no human intervention whatsoever. This is a good way to augment an organization's need to be able to frequently merge newly developed codes with main code lines. At this phase, an organization's code base is in a constant state of ready deployment.

Continuous Deployment: This shouldn't be confused with the previous phase, continuous delivery. This is considered to be the most advanced DevOps phase and is a condition wherein organizations are able to deploy programs or codes directly to production without the need for any kind of human assistance. As such, it's considered to be the "nirvana" of DevOps and this makes companies "unicorns."

Teams that make use of continuous delivery never deploy codes that aren't tested. Instead, they run new codes through a series of automated testing procedures prior to pushing them to the production line. Typically, only a small percentage of users get to receive newly released codes where an automated feedback system is used to monitor usage and quality of the code prior to full release.

As mentioned earlier, only a few companies are already in this phase – the **nirvana phase** – of DevOps because doing so takes time and serious resources. But given that most organizations find continuous integration quite a lofty goal, many often aim for continuous delivery instead.

The Focus of DevOps

Establishing a culture of collaboration and using automation (with DevOps tools) as a means to improve an organization's efficiency are the main focus of DevOps. While there's a tendency to be biased towards either tools or culture, the truth is it takes some combination of both tools and culture for an organization to become optimally productive.

Culture

When talking about culture within the context of DevOps, the point of focus is on increasing collaboration, reducing isolation of units (silos), sharing the responsibilities, increasing each team's autonomy, increasing quality, putting a premium on feedback and raising the level of automation. Most of what DevOps values are the same as those of the Agile system because it's an extension of the latter. We'll talk more about Agile later on but in a nutshell,

Agile may be considered as a holistic software delivery system that measures progress through working software. Under Agile, developers, product owners, UX people, and testers all work as a tight-knit unit to achieve a common goal.

As an extension of the Agile system, DevOps involves adding an operations' mindset – and possibly a team member with some operational responsibilities – to the team. In the past, the progress of DevOps was measured in terms of working software. These days, it's measured in terms of working software that's already in the hands of the end users or customers. This is achieved only through shared system (runs the software) maintenance responsibilities, close collaboration via breaking down of silos or obstacles to such collaboration and preparation of the software so that it'll run in the system with high delivery automation and quality feedback.

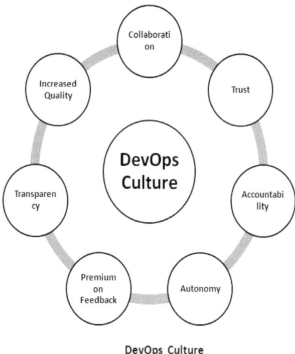

DevOps Culture

Tools

When talking about DevOps tools, we talk about configuration management, building and testing of systems, deployment of applications, control over different versions of the program or code, and tools for monitoring quality and progress. Each of the maturity

34

phases of DevOps – continuous integration, delivery, and deployment – all need a different set of tools. While it's true that there are tools commonly used in all the phases, the number and kinds of tools needed increase as an organization moves up through the chain of delivery.

And speaking of tools, some of the most important ones include:

Source Code Repository: This refers to a place where codes are checked in and changed by developers. The repository manages the different iterations of code that are checked in it, making it possible for developers to avoid working on each other's works. Some of the most popular tools used as code repository include **TFS, Bitbucket, Cloudforce, Subversion and Grit.**

Build Server: This refers to an automation tool that collects code in the source code repository into an executable code base. Some of the most popular tools include **Artifactory, SonarQube, and Jenkins.**

Configuration Management: This defines how an environment or a server is configured. Popular tools include **Chef and Puppet**.

Virtual Infrastructure: This type of infrastructure lets organizations create new machines using configuration management tools like **Chef and Puppet**. These infrastructures are provided by cloud-vending companies that sell platform as a service (PaaS) or infrastructure and include Microsoft's Azure and Amazon Web Services. Organizations can also get "private clouds", which are private virtual infrastructures that allow fur running a cloud on top of the hardware in an organization's data center. An example of this is **vCloud by VMware.**

When combined with automation tools, virtual infrastructures can help empower organizations that use DevOps to configure their servers with no need for human intervention. An organization can test brand new codes simply by sending them to their cloud infrastructure, creating the necessary environment, and running all necessary tests with no need for any human fingers to touch a computer's keyboards.

Test Automation: When doing DevOps testing, the focus is on automated testing to make sure that only fully deployable or working codes are deployed to production. Without an extensive automated testing strategy, it's hard – if not downright impossible – to achieve a state of continuous delivery with no human intervention where organizations can be confident about the codes they deploy into production. Some of the most popular tools for test automation include **Water and Selenium**.

Pipeline Orchestration: Think of a pipeline as a factory assembly line. Further, think of this as the time when the development team finishes writing

the code until the code is fully deployed
in production.

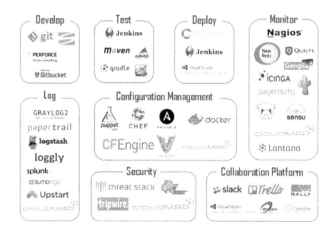

Source of above image: emaze.com

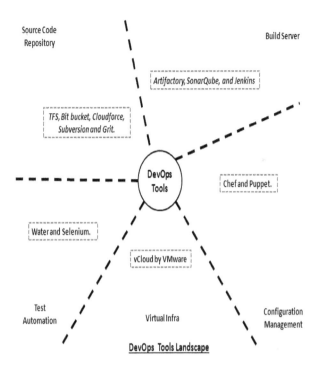

DevOps Tools Landscape

3. The DevOps Evolution

Many organizations have experienced much success when it comes to using Agile methods for hastening the delivery of software. Starting from the development organization, Agile has slowly increased its scope to include other important areas like operations and information technology (IT). Teams and sub-teams have learned how to streamline processes, improve the quality of feedback mechanisms and how to speed up the innovation processes in IT departments. All of these have had significant effects on organizations' productivity.

To capitalize on these developments, continuous delivery and DevOps were created with the aim of connecting organizations' development teams with IT operations primarily via automated systems. By doing so, organizations were able to foster an environment of increased the responsiveness, agility and faster software delivery times to the market.

Back in 2001, a document called **The Agile Manifesto** emerged from the software development environment and introduced what is now called as Agile Development. Methodologies based on the Agile system oriented software developers in the art of breaking down the software development process into much smaller bites that are called "user stories". These "stories" helped speed up feedback acquisition processes, which in turn helped organizations align their products' features with the needs of their markets much faster.

Agile focused on helping small teams and developers work much more efficiently and smarter. At first, only small software startup companies who were excited to disrupt what was then the current software market and who were willing to do that through trial and error were into the Agile system. As the process gradually evolved and matured, the whole software community started to become more and more responsive and accepting of methodologies based on the Agile system.

In turn, such increasing acceptance made the concept of "scale" more and more important in the industry. Developers were able to come out with functioning programs or software codes much faster. But when it come to the downstream processes of testing and deployment of newly developed codes, two things prevented organizations from increasing the turnaround or delivery times of quality software to their intended users: fragmented processes and the existence of functional silos, i.e., segregated operating business units.

Eventually, the Agile system gave birth to new technologies and processes that were aimed at automating and streamlining the whole cycle of software delivery. With the coming of age of continuous integration or CI, smaller and more frequent code releases became the norm as more and more codes needed to be tested and integrated daily. This in turn put a huge strain on Quality Assurance (QA) and Operations (Ops) teams.

A breakthrough book by Jez Humble titled Continuous Delivery helped promote the idea that the entire software lifecycle can be viewed as one automatable process. It was so effective in promoting said idea that even Fortune 1000 companies started embracing this idea. In turn, the perceived value of Agile initiatives that were at the time blocked and stalled and in the process, also helped increase the stakes for treating software delivery as a crucial and strategic initiative in business.

Agile focused on the needs of code developers. On the other hand, continuous delivery and DevOps initiatives helped organizations become much more efficient, productive, and profitable. These two have also helped organizations improve their software delivery cycles.

Many industry experts believe that DevOps and CD – as Agile system extensions – have the biggest chance for organizations to optimize their enterprise values. An industry expert once said about CD that if the software delivery cycle is a concert, Agile is the opening act and CD is the show's main performer.

Software-driven organizations that continue to evolve in terms of technical frameworks and processes have already transitioned from just implementing continuous integration to continuous delivery. In doing so, CD has transformed software delivery as we know it and has extended the potential of Agile by linking DevOps practices and tools with CI or continuous integration.

Continuous delivery is – from a technical viewpoint – a collection of methodologies and practices that are focused on improving software delivery processes and optimize the reliability of organizations' software releases. It makes use of automation – from continuous integration builds all the way to deployment of codes – and involves all aspects of research and development and operations organization. At the end, CD helps organizations release quality software systematically, repeatedly and more frequently to their end users or customers.

Leading software expert Martin Fowler developed key tenets for Agile-based continuous delivery, based on successful agile methodologies. He outlined key questions to ask in continuous delivery such as:

- Can the organization readily deploy your software through its entire lifecycle?
- Can the organization keep the software deployable and prioritize it even while working on its new features?
- Is it possible for anyone to receive quick and automated feedback about their applications and infrastructures' production readiness whenever a person modifies or changes them?
- Is it possible for the organization to just push a button to deploy

any version of software whenever it's needed?

Extending the Agile system through continuous delivery provides organizations several benefits including:
- A faster time to deploy software to the market;
- Better quality of products;
- Higher customer satisfaction;
- Higher productivity and efficiency;
- Increased reliability for software releases; and
- The capability to create the right products.

Agile's impact in the software industry has been both highly disruptive and far-reaching. It has also helped promote new ideas outside of itself, which includes multi-functional processes (DevOps) as well as continuous delivery (CD) that impact both software end users and organizations. With the onset of DevOps and CD, waterfall approaches have been archived in the annals of software history and communication and collaboration continue to remain important aspects of an organization's operations.

Timeline

For a better understanding of the evolution of DevOps and CD, here's a timeline of crucial events in their development.

2007

A software development consultant by the name of Patrick Debois tried to learn all of IT's aspects. Within 15 years, Patrick has assumed quite a number of different roles in the Information Technology sector so that he can work in just about every role imaginable within an IT organization, the goal of which was to get a holistic yet intimate understanding of Information Technology. Developer, system administrator, network specialist, project manager, and tester – you name it and Patrick Debois has worked it.

In 2007, Patrick took on a consulting job for a huge data migration center organization and was in charge of testing. That meant he spent a huge chunk of his time working with development and operations (DevOps). For the longest time, Patrick had been uneasy about how differently Devs and Ops worked. In particular, he became frustrated with the way work was managed between these two groups when it came to data migration.

That time, CI or continuous integration was starting to become very popular within the Agile circle and was brining development ever so closer to deployment. Still, there was a void when it came to bridging the huge gap between Dev and Ops. At this point, Debois had a strong sense of sureness that there has got to be a much better way for these two particular groups to work much better.

2008

Patrick chanced upon a post at the 2008 Agile Conference by Andrew Shafer, wherein the idea for a session that'll discuss an agile infrastructure. After seeing the post, Patrick attended the session but unfortunately, the idea was very badly received to the point that only Patrick showed up. Not even Andrew Shafer, the brains behind the idea, bothered to show up at the session he himself called for!

But that didn't stop or discouraged Patrick Debois. With his enthusiasm over knowing he wasn't alone with his ideas or point of view concerning the divide between Dev and Ops exceeding that of a kid in a candy store, he ultimately tracked Andrew Shafer down and formed a Google group named Agile System Administration.

2009

Flickr's Senior VP for Technical Operations John Allspaw and Director For Engineering Paul Hammond presented "10 + Deploys Per Day: Dev and Ops Cooperation At Flickr" at the 2009 O'Reilly Velocity Conference in San Jose. This presentation provided what will ultimately become the groundwork for improving software deployment via improvements in the way Dev and Ops work together.

Though Patrick was in Belgium at the time of the presentation, he was able to catch it via live streaming. This presentation encouraged him to come up with his own conference in Ghent, Belgium: DevsOpsDays. This conference was able to gather together a very lively group of futuristic thinkers who are passionate about how to improve software development. Even more important is that the group maintained and publicized the conversation over Twitter using #DevOpsDays as its hashtag. In an attempt to optimize Twitter's limited character limit, the group eventually truncated the hashtag into #DevOps.

2010

In 2010, the DevOpsDays conferences were held in the United States and Australia. The conference was conducted in more countries and cities all over the world over time. And this fostered even more face-to-face meeting between like minded IT people, which in turn made more IT people excited about the idea of DevOps until it came to a point that DevOps became a full-fledged grassroots movement.

2011

Prior to 2011, the grassroots movement known as DevOps was primarily driven by open source tools and individuals with hardly any attention from software vendors and analysts. But on that year, DevOps started infiltrating the mainstream by getting the attention of top analysts such as Jay Lyman and Cameron Haight from 451 Research and Gartner, respectively. As a result, the big boys of the software industry started to take notice and even market DevOps.

2012

DevOps – at this time – was fast becoming a buzzword in the industry. As a result, the DevOpsDays conference continued with its growth all over the world.

2013

By this time, several authors have begun writing books on DevOps as a result of the growing insatiable public thirst for information related to DevOps. Some of these authors include Mary and Tom Poppendiek with Implementing Lean Software Development, and Gene Kim, Kevin Behr and George Spafford with The Phoenix Project.

2014

Some of the world's biggest companies started to incorporate DevOps into their organization.   These include Lego, Nordstrom and Target.

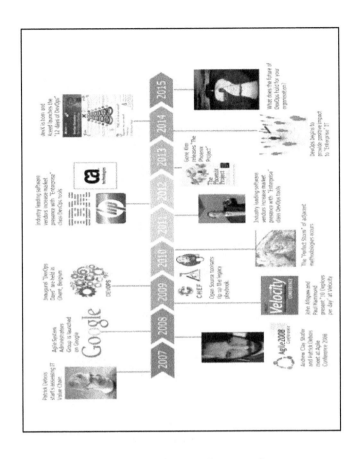

Source: Article "Evolution of DevOps" on LinkedIn

4. The Agile System and DevOps/CD

From out of the need to keep up with the increasing speed at which software is developed and the increasing number of software being developed and released as a result of such increasing speed, which Agile methods have allowed organizations to achieve, came forth the DevOps. It may be considered as the love child of Agile software development, as significant advancements in methods and culture through the years have brought to fore the need for an approach to the entire software delivery cycle that's more holistic.

What Is The Agile System?

The Agile system or Agile Development is a general word used to refer to numerous incremental and iterative software development methodologies. Among these methodologies, the most popular ones **are Extreme Programming (XP), Lean Development, Scaled Agile Framework (SAF), Kanban, and Scrum.**

Despite each methodology having their own unique approach, all of them have common threads – vision and core values. All of them basically incorporate continuous feedback and iteration for successfully refining and eventually, delivering a software system. All of them also involve continuous planning, testing, integration, and other kinds of continuous evolution both in terms of the software and the projects. All of them are also lightweight compared to other old-school approaches or processes such as Waterfall-type ones. Also, these methodologies are naturally adaptable. But the most important commonality among these Agile methods is the ability to empower people to quickly and effectively collaborate and make decisions together.

At first, developers made up most Agile teams. As these teams started to become more and more efficient and effective in producing software, it became obvious that having separate development (Dev) and quality assurance (QA) teams was an inefficient way of doing things. As a result, Agile methodologies started to encompass the QA process so that the speed at which software is delivered can be much faster. Agile continues to grow, which now includes delivery and support members, so that Agile can encompass all aspects from ideation to delivery of software.

The ideals of DevOps are able to extend the development practices of Agile through the rationalization of how software moves through all stages – building, validating, deployment, and delivery. It does so while empowering cross-functional units or teams by giving them complete ownership of the software application process from design through production support.

DevOps and Agile

Essentially, DevOps is simply the expansion of principles used by Agile. It includes systems and operations and doesn't just stop dealing with concerns once codes are checked in. Aside from collaborating as a cross-functional unit made up of developers, testers, and designers that comprise an Agile team, DevOps also includes operations people in its cross-functional units. This is because instead of just focusing on coming up with a software that works, which is what Agile's all about, DevOps aims to provide customers with a complete service, i.e., a working software that's effectively and efficiently delivered to its end users or customers. DevOps emphasizes the need to minimize or even eliminate obstacles and barriers to effective collaboration between software developers and operations (end users), making the most out of their combined skills.

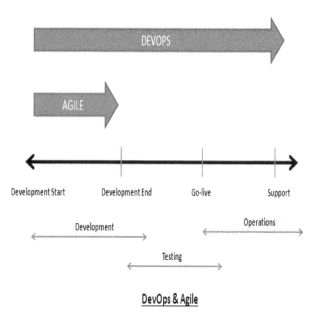

DevOps & Agile

While Agile teams make use of automated building, automation testing, continuous integration and continuous delivery, DevOps extends Agile teams a bit more to include "infrastructure as code", metrics, monitoring, configuration management and a tool chain perspective to cloud computing, virtualization, and tooling in order to speed up changes inside the world of modern infrastructure. Also, DevOps incorporates other tools like

58

orchestration (e.g., zookeeper, mesos, and noah), configuration management (e.g., cfengine, ansible, chef, and puppet), containerization, virtualization and monitoring (e.g., docker, vagrant, OpenStack and AWS), and many others.

As you can see, DevOps is merely an extension of the Agile system that encompasses operations in its definition of cross-functional Agile teams and fosters collaboration between developers and operations in order to fully deliver working software to their end users.

5. Scrum

Scrum refers to an Agile methodology or framework for managing projects that's primarily used for projects involving software development, the goals of which are to deliver new software features or capabilities every other week or month. Scrum is one approach that heavily influenced the document known as the Agile Manifesto that enunciates a particular set of principles and values that help guide organizations make decisions related to the faster development of high-quality software.

The use of Scrum has already encompassed other business activities such as marketing and information technology, where projects need to move along in complex and ambiguous environments. Many leadership teams also use Scrum as their Agile management method, usually mixing it with Kanban and lean practices.

Scrum and Agile

Scrum may be considered as a sub-type of the Agile software development system. Agile, if you may recall, is comprised of principles and values that describe an organization's daily activities and interactions. In and by itself, Agile is neither specific nor prescriptive.

Scrum adheres to Agile's principles and values but also includes further specifications and definitions. In particular, these additions pertain to specific practices concerning the development of software. And while Scrum was developed for Agile software development, it has become a preferred framework by which Agile projects in general are managed. Occasionally, Scrum is also called Scrum development or Scrum project management.

Some of the benefits of using Scrum include:

- Better satisfaction among stakeholders;
- Faster time to market;
- Happier members or employees;
- Higher quality products;
- Improved dynamics between teams and members; and
- Increased productivity.

This methodology can address work complexities by among other things, more transparent data or information. Through improved transparency, the organization's stakeholders can check and if necessary, adjust or adapt depending on the current or actual condition or environment the organization's in instead of projected conditions or environments. This ability to check and adjust lets organizations or teams to work on many of the common shortcomings of waterfall development processes, which include among others:
- Confusion as a result of frequently changing requirements;
- Inaccurate reporting of progress;

- Software quality compromises; and
- Underestimating of costs, resources, and time.

In Scrum software development, transparency in common standards and terms is a must so that delivered software meets expectations. Inspecting frequently helps to ensure continuous progress and help the organization detect any unwanted variations in results early enough to enable quick and timely adjustments. When it comes to inspection and adaptation, the most popular Scrum events include Sprint Planning, Stand Ups (a.k.a., daily Scrum), Sprint Retrospective and Sprint Review.

Scrum Components

The Scrum Agile development methodology is made up of key components: team roles, ceremonies (events), artifacts, and rules. Normally, scrum teams are made up of 5 to 9 members with no specific team leader who decides how to attack a specific problem or who delegates project tasks. Decision-making is a collegial process, i.e., the whole team – as a unit – gets to make decisions regarding solutions to problems and issues faced by the team. Every Scrum team member plays an essential part in coming up with solutions to problems faced by the team and is anticipated to bring a product all the way from conception to finalization.

In Scrum teams, members can take on 3 roles, namely that of a product owner, Scrum master, and the development team. A product owner is a project's primary stakeholder. Normally, a product owner is an external or internal customer, or a customer's representative. There can only be one product owner and he or she determines or communicates the project's overall mission and vision that the team is expected to build or develop. Ultimately, the product owner's accountable for taking care of product backlogs and accepting finished work increments.

The ScrumMaster role is assigned to a person who will serve as the product owner, development team, and organization's servant leader. The ScrumMaster acts more like a facilitator considering the lack of hierarchical authority over development teams, and ensures the team's adherence to Scrum rules, practices, and theories. He or she also protects the development team by doing everything he or she can to assist the team in optimizing its performance. "Everything" may include things like helping the product owner manage backlogs, facilitate meetings and remove obstacles or impediments.

The Development Team is a cross-functional unit that's self-organizing and is equipped with all the necessary skills for delivering shippable increments every time a sprint or iteration is completed. Under the Scrum methodology, the role "developer" expands to include the role of any person involved in the process of creating the content for delivery. For members of the development team, there are no titles and there's no one who tells the team how to convert backlog items into increments that can already be shipped to customers.

Ceremonies (Scrum Events)

A sprint refers to a time-boxed period in which particular types of work are finished and are prepared for review. Normally, sprints last for 2 to 4 weeks but it's not impossible to hear of sprints that conclude within 1 week only.

Sprint planning refers to team meetings that are also time-bound or boxed. These help determine which among a product's backlog items will be shipped to the end user and how to actually do it.

Daily Stand Ups refer to very short meetings not exceeding 15 minutes. In said meetings, each member of the team covers progress made in the project since the last stand up in a fast and transparent manner, any obstacles that are hindering him or her from progressing in the project and any work planned prior to the next meeting.

Sprint reviews refer to events where in the development team gets the opportunity to demonstrate or present completed work during sprints. Here, the product owner checks the work vs. pre-determined criterion for acceptance and based on such criterion, approves or rejects the finished work. Here, the clients and stakeholders also provide valuable feedback that ensures each and every increment delivered is up to the customer's needs and specifications.

Retro – a.k.a. the retrospective – refers to the final team meeting during the sprint to find out the things that went well, those that went bad, and how the development team can further improve its performance in succeeding sprints. This meeting's attended by the team members and the ScrumMaster and is a crucial opportunity for the team to set its sights on improving overall performance and determine continuous improvement strategies for its processes.

Artifacts or Documents

Scrum artifacts include product backlogs, sprint backlogs, and increments. A product backlog is possibly the most valuable Scrum document or artifact, which lists every product, project, or system requirement. The product backlog may be viewed as a list of things to do, where each item on the list is equated with a deliverable that provides business value. These items are ordered or ranked according to their business value by the product owner.

A sprint backlog refers to a list of items sourced from the product backlog. In particular, these items are those that need to be completed in a sprint or iteration.

Increments are the sum of all product backlogs that have already been addressed or completed from the time the latest software version was released. The product owner decides when to release increments but it's the team's responsibility to ensure everything that comes with an increment is ready for release. These ready-for-release items are also referred to as Potentially Shippable Increments or PSIs.

Scrum Rules

When it comes to rules that govern Scrum, they're entirely up to the team and should be determined by what is best for their particular processes. The most competent Agile coaches will instruct teams to begin with some of the most basic Scrum events discussed earlier and then review and adapt according the team's particular needs. Doing so ensures continuous improvements in how teams collaborate.

6. Kanban

Kanban is a way of managing the product creation process. It emphasizes continuous delivery (CD) without having to overburden an organization's development (Dev) team. It's also designed to improve collaboration between an organization's different units. Kanban is based on 3 key principles:

- Visualization of the things done today, i.e., the workflow. The ability to see everything within the context of each other can provide a lot of useful information to the organization.
- Limiting the amount of work-in-progress (WIP), this helps bring balance to a flow-based approach that helps an organization's teams avoid taking on too much work all at once.
- Flow enhancement, i.e., as soon as a task is done, work is started on the next highest order task from the backlog queue.

Consistent with DevOps and CD, Kanban helps promote ongoing collaborations and promotes active and continuous learning and improvement by defining an optimal team workflow. And for any DevOps initiative, the implicit goals are fast movement, rapid deployment, and responsiveness to a rapidly changing business environment. Kanban – as a methodology – is a very helpful and progressive tool for achieving an organization's desired outcome. In particular, the ability to be able to monitor an organization's progress and status on a daily basis instead of weekly isn't just a very appealing proposition but one that can also transform the way an organization is able to communicate and complete its tasks.

The Kanban approach or methodology helps developers work as one solid unit and finish everything they've started. If through the Kanban principle on limited Work-In-Progress a part of the development team is obligated to allocate their resources into other aspects of an ongoing project to assist in its completion, these members will be able to see the project from a larger and different perspective. This can be helpful in identifying possible issues, obstacles and bottlenecks even before they manifest and cause problems.

The ability to see projects from a holistic point of view by as much of its stakeholders as possible helps teams and the organization to adapt a system-level view. Within the underpinning principles of DevOps, this is referred to as the first way, the outcomes of which include:
- Known defects are never passed to downstream work centers;
- Local optimizations are never allowed to create global degradation;
- Continuous seeking of increased work flow;
- Continuous seeking of deeper and more profound understanding of the system; and

- Removal of the "time box" out of the equation.

Using a Kanban approach to the DevOps movement is one that requires nerves of steel because it's relatively new compared to its other Agile brothers, particularly Scrum. As such, there's much discussion about how it's more appropriate for initiatives that are time-critical like a change management endeavor or a product launch that's happening in 7 days' time. Regardless, the Kanban methodology is still one that's worth taking into consideration and checking to determine potentially beneficial changes that it may bring to an organization, specifically to its workflow. More importantly, the Kanban methodology can help an organization determine whether or not it's close to violating acceptable WIP limits. But the biggest gains that can be enjoyed from using Kanban is in finding an organization's work process constraints.

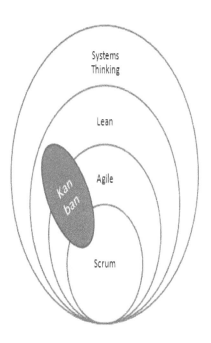

Agile Scrum & Kanban

7. Kanban versus Scrum

With Scrum, product owners only have a limited amount of time to incorporate user stories into a sprint, which is between 2 to 3 weeks. This however poses a problem – unusual breaking points are created for people who deploy and test the software. Too little stories may not result in shippable products towards the end of an iteration or sprint, may increase dependence between sprints or iterations, and may lead to very challenging coordination efforts and very difficult testing.

Using the Kanban approach on the other hand, frees up product owners from any time limitations. This is because the Kanban methodology is all about focusing on the most significant work and getting them done through processes to the right people and at the right times.

To get a better idea of the differences between the Scrum and Kanban Agile methodologies, let's take a look at two of its most crucial differences: rules and workflow.

Rules

Both the Scrum and Kanban software development methods have rules governing the performance of work. The Scrum method is the more prescriptive of the two. There are 23 mandatory and 12 optional rules for Scrum implementation per Agile Advice, which include:

- Daily meetings must be held;
- During iterations or sprints, no interruptions are allowed;
- Product owners should create and manage a backlog of its products;
- Progress should be measured using a burn-down chart;
- Teams must be cross-functional; and
- Time for work is boxed.

Collectively, such rules make for quite a rigid system in which teams must work to successfully implement Scrum in their software development. There are 2 major challenges to this. One is called ScrumBut, i.e., organizations use "Scrum, but..." This means many organizations – due to the methodology's rigidity – tend to ignore some of the methodologies rules, which leads to a non-optimal use of the Scrum framework.

The other challenge presented here is the time box, which are great for distraction-less working time for software developers to deliver specific products, and providing regular bases for stakeholders by which to steer and evaluate projects. But looking at it from the lenses of DevOps, workflow is regularly broken by specific software delivery checkpoints or milestones. Such disruption in workflow makes it challenging for organizations to coordinate sprint dependencies and ensure successful transfer of software from development to production.

When you evaluate the Kanban software development methodology, you'll find that it's substantially less restrictive. Consider it only has 2 rules, which are:
- Workflow visualization; and
- Setting limits to amount of work-in-progress.

Yep – that's all folks! Having only 2 rules, this methodology is a very open and flexible one, which can be easily utilized under any environment. In some organizations, Kanban is even used outside of software development, from product manufacturing to marketing! You can even incorporate some of Scrum's work rules into Kanban if you so desire. That's how flexible it is.

Because Kanban focuses more on the workflow instead of time boxes, it's the better choice for utilizing with DevOps. Because Kanban emphasizes the optimization of the whole software delivery process instead of just the development phase, many software development experts think it's the perfect "spouse" for DevOps.

Workflow

The other major difference between Kanban and Scrum is the workflow. This particular difference is an offshoot of the difference in its rules. With Scrum, you choose the features that need to completed in the next sprint beforehand. Afterwards, the sprint or iteration is "locked," the work is performed over the sprint's duration (usually in a couple of weeks), and at the sprint's end, the cue is vacant or empty. By locking the sprint in, the work team is assured of ample and necessary time for working on a problem without any interruptions from other seemingly urgent requirements. At the end of each iteration or sprint, feedback sessions help stakeholders approve or disapprove work that's already been delivered and steer the project depending on changes in the organization's activities or environment.

When using the Kanban methodology for developing software, an organization isn't subject to sprint time constraints. Instead, the much focus is given on ensuring that workflow remains uninterrupted and without any known issues as it moves downstream.

Limits, however, are placed on the amount of work queued or in progress under the Kanban methodology. It means that at any given point time in the software delivery cycle, the team can only work on a certain number of issues or features. In setting such a limit, teams are compelled to focus on only a few work items on hand, which often leads to high quality work.

A visible workflow fosters a sense of urgency for teams to keep things moving. Keep in mind that the Kanban methodology was a product of manufacturing genius and as such, its focus is on efficiency and productivity. And as it's extended to the software development arena, it incorporates important aspects of software development success like participation of stakeholders.

DevOps, Kanban, and Scrum

For organizations use DevOps, increased efficiencies, more frequent deployment of features, and high responsiveness to business demands are some of their most important goals. As such, each of the two methods can help organizations address various areas of their DevOps better than the other. While Kanban seems to be all the rage these days, it's not necessarily the automatic choice for organizations.

If an organization is responsible for developing new features that need stakeholder feedback and high developer focus, then Scrum is possibly the better choice for its DevOps. In this scenario, Scrum's sprint lock feature and demos for stakeholders at the end of each sprint or iteration can be very, very valuable to the organization.

If an organization is accountable for simple maintenance and is more reactive than the regular organization, Kanban may be the better option. This is because it has greater flexibility in terms of responding to stakeholder feedback and it doesn't require locking of backlogs.

At the end of the day, every organization's different and as such, they should know their teams' strengths and areas for improvements in order to choose the best software development method. At some point, it may even be optimal to get the best of both methodologies and combine them into one for the optimal achievement of an organization's goals.

8. Organizational Culture Change for DevOps Success

DevOps started as a method for developing software, which was intended to hasten the software building, testing, and release processes by making two crucial teams – Operations (Ops) and Developers (Dev) – collaborate more effectively. In effect, this has to do with organizational culture.

But how exactly does organizational culture play a big role in successful employment of DevOps in organizations, particularly within tech organizations? Lucas Welch of Chef explains this by giving his working definition of DevOps, which is a professional and cultural movement that focuses on how high velocity organizations are built and operated, which is derived from its practitioner's personal experiences. He explains further that tech companies need to provide their employees a safe enough environment, enough freedom, and access to knowledge when needed if they want to succeed in a DevOps environment. Further, he explains that its team members must be empowered to think, speak, and ask without restraint or hindrance in order for them to quickly act. When done correctly, this type of collaboration among teams helps empower and engage team members with a purpose, aligned leadership, and shared sets of beliefs and values.

However, it's easier to talk about the integration of 2 teams with totally different subcultures than to actually integrate them. Based on a research done by Gartner, out of the 75% of IT departments that would've tried to come up with a bi-modal capacity by the year 2018, only less than 50% will enjoy the benefits that come along with using new software development techniques like DevOps. And according to Gartner's Research Director Ian Head, up to 90%

of I&O organizations that try to use DevOps without first addressing their particular cultural foundations will eventually fail.

DevOps discussions appear to be about some new concept and methodology, but they have been circulating in the industry for long now. It's just that such concepts have gone around using different names.

But this doesn't do anything to reduce the value of the DevOps movement. Tech companies have started to get that focusing on improving collaboration between businesses units that seem to lie on opposite poles of the organization can lead to increased productivity and product quality.

Often times, the challenge in changing an organization's culture to suit DevOps are shifting the focus from the technical side of DevOps to the cultural aspect of it. It has been realized across board that organizational culture change is the most important factor for maximizing improvements from adapting this methodology.

Things to Consider

In order to successfully change an organization's culture for optimization of DevOps benefits, the following should be considered:

Dialogue Space: An organization must be able to provide a space or venue where all parties involved in DevOps can meet and talk. It shouldn't be a surprise to find that when people are asked to change the way they operate in terms of performing their functions within the organization, they'd feel anxious and resistant – at least in the beginning. An organization can help provide a very good foundation for transitions like these by giving members who'll be affected by the implementation of DevOps opportunities to interface with one another in an environment that's safe and secure so that they can fully grasp the need for DevOps implementation. The organization can also ensure proper clarification of roles, responsibilities, and interdependencies to help affected members feel secure and at peace with the implementation of DevOps because often times, ignorance is the source of anxieties and insecurities.

Leader Support. An organization's leaders are some of the key stakeholders when it comes to transitioning into DevOps and as such, it must be able to provide the necessary support for them – i.e., tools, abilities, skills, and knowledge – that will enable them to lead other members through a successful transition to DevOps. Sadly, many organizations make the fatal mistake of assuming that their leaders already know what to do and have all the necessary skill sets for the job at hand. Organizations only realize such mistakes during transition, when leaders are unable to successfully lead their teams and in the process, hamper the entire transition process.

Stakeholder Engagement: In certain ways, DevOps needs key groups or teams in the organization to change their current perspectives, assumptions, and beliefs concerning how to best get their works done. By getting these groups or teams involved in the process of redefining their work along the lines of DevOps, organizations can help make them see that they are important parts of the change to be implemented instead of feeling that the organization is doing something nasty to them.

Accept Mistakes: When an organization asks their key people – most if not all of whom already have deeply-entrenched career identities – to change the way they see and think about collaborating with others to achieve a new common goal, hiccups are bound to happen despite the best laid plans and preparations to avoid them. Simply put, mistakes will happen along the way and what's more important and realistic is for an organization's leadership to react properly towards these situations because this will affect how people involved in the DevOps transition will move forward. If leaders immediately use punishment as a means of rectifying mistakes and hopefully preventing their recurrence, there's a high risk that team members will go back to their familiar place of safety – their old ways of doing things. If the organization's leaders can use mistake moments as opportunities for teaching members the proper way of doing DevOps and learn to live with such mistakes as a normal part of doing something new, the organization will be able to rebound from hiccups and glitches much faster and achieve full DevOps implementation at the soonest possible time.

Cynicism Vs. Skepticism: Skepticism in light of being presented with crucial new information about how to best get work done is normal. Consider the fact that when people have been doing their work for so many years with hardly any changes, certain key beliefs and assumptions of how to do their jobs and how to collaborate with others in the performance of their jobs become as hard as cement. So when DevOps is initially presented to them, it's ok for them to be skeptical about it. But over time, their minds will gradually change as they see the great benefits of implementing DevOps. But cynicism is an altogether different beast. While the minds of skeptics are open to the possibility of being convinced otherwise, cynics are hard set on what they think and believe to be true and as a result, they normally reject all claims contrary or not in line with their current belief systems. If skeptics believe in "guilty until proven innocent", cynics believe "immediately guilty regardless of evidences to the contrary that may be presented later on...period!" Organizations will be better off identifying the cynics in their teams and excluding them from DevOps transition and full implementation when possible.

Time: Everything worth doing successfully takes time. The only difference is how much time is needed. It's the same with organizations that are transitioning to DevOps and embedding it as part of an organization's new culture. As team members start to see more and more of DevOps benefits as time goes by, the more they'll naturally be aligned to its principles and practices. At a certain point in time, DevOps will become a natural part of an organization's culture. A fatal mistake would be to expect DevOps to be fully integrated and ingrained in an organization's culture very quickly. Doing so will lead to frustration and drastic corrective measures that can sabotage efforts instead of maximizing them.

A Holistic Approach

At the very center, DevOps is all about collaboration and teamwork. And that can only happen when people's hearts and minds are generally – not perfectly – in sync. That is the power of culture and when an organization is able to successfully foster a culture of collaboration and openness to change, then successful transition to and implementation of DevOps is not far behind.

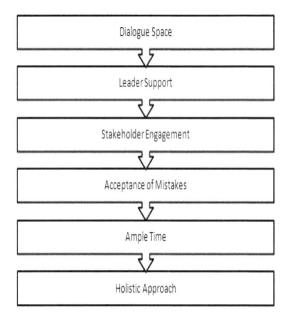

Factors for Organizational Change to adopt DevOps

9. DevOps Ecosystem and emerging trends

Refer the below line:

"Only 10% of companies describe themselves as fully digital." – **Datum**

Any organization, big technology firm or a small e-commerce firm, all are aiming to be fully digital. While there is a major focus on the disruptive technologies which would lead the next digital wave; the modus operandi of its execution is equally important. The true Digital Transformation can be achieved by creating DevOps culture and environment.

The DevOps Environment

DevOps is an environment, not a technology. Designing, Developing, Deploying, and Operating in a unified environment is the key aspect of DevOps methodology. Continuous deployment and integration facilitates the faster rate of software development, testing and operations. Efficiency and automation are the major pillars of this methodology.

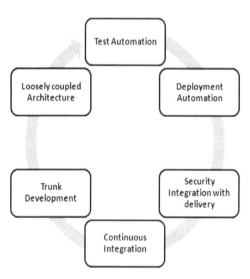

Factors creating positive DevOps Environment

To explain it further,

Automation

Automation allows the high performers of the system to focus more on innovation rather than operational activities. One example could be cited of transformation at HP LaserJet. On the way to transformation, the organization followed continuous delivery practice and invested in automation (major focus on automated testing). This resulted in multiple fold increase in time invested in developing new features or innovation.

Trunk Development

A model, where developers' works on software code in a single branch called 'trunk' and they resist creating other long standing development branches by practicing techniques. They avoid any merger step and do not break the continuity.

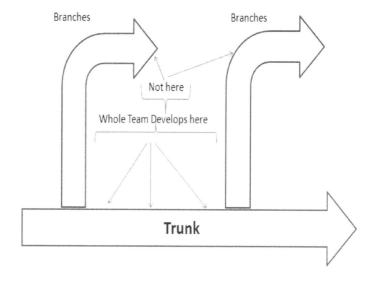

Practically, developers work in small high performing teams and develop off the trunk (on branches). The pragmatic way for best delivery performance could be:

- Daily merger of code into trunk.
- Branches with day log or less lifetimes
- Three or less active branches.

DevOps Architecture (Loosely Coupled)

Continuous delivery is driven greatly by the team and architecture which are loosely coupled. Loosely coupled team can complete their tasks independently. Similarly, loosely coupled architecture is the one where any modification can be done in the individual component or service without making changes in the dependent services or components.

The loosely coupled architecture results in strong IT and organizational performance because the delivery team can perform testing and deployment without depending on other teams for any work or approvals. It also avoids back- and – forth communication, making the process smooth and efficient.

Overall, it can be stated that more than automation of test and deployment process; the flexibility provided by loosely coupled architecture contributes towards continuous delivery.

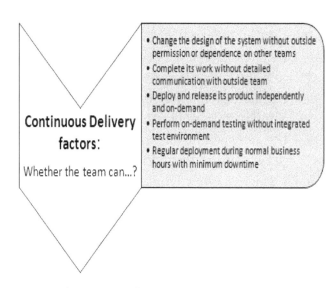

Continuous Delivery factors:

Whether the team can…?

- Change the design of the system without outside permission or dependence on other teams
- Complete its work without detailed communication with outside team
- Deploy and release its product independently and on-demand
- Perform on-demand testing without integrated test environment
- Regular deployment during normal business hours with minimum downtime

Emerging Trends in DevOps

1. **Containers and Micro services would be integrated big time with DevOps:**"One of the major factors impacting DevOps is the shift towards micro services," says Arvind Soni, VP of product at Netsil

✓ **Microservices:** It is a application development

architecture where applications are developed independently and are deployable, modular and small. Also, each modular service runs unique process and communicates in a defined manner serving business goals.

✓ **Containers:** It is an operating system virtualization method that facilitates application to run in resource isolated process. So, the application is deployed quickly, reliably and consistently in any deployment environment.

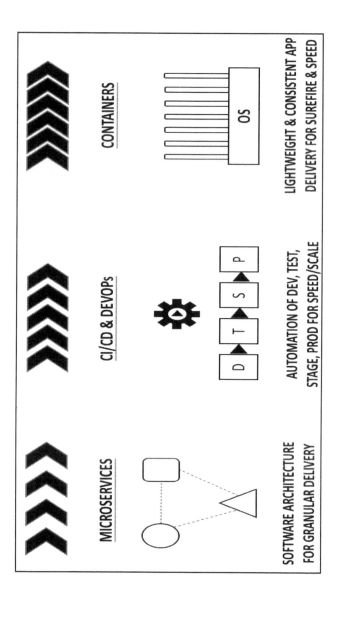

MICROSERVICES

CI/CD & DEVOPs

CONTAINERS

D → T → S → P

OS

SOFTWARE ARCHITECTURE FOR GRANULAR DELIVERY

AUTOMATION OF DEV, TEST, STAGE, PROD FOR SPEED/SCALE

LIGHTWEIGHT & CONSISTENT APP DELIVERY FOR SUREFIRE & SPEED

2. **Expert teams practicing DevOps would cut down on security nets**: It may be the case that expert DevOps teams may decide to no longer have pre-production environment. The team may be confident and the process of deploying and testing in staging environment may be avoided. Again this may be the case with expert teams who are confident to **identify, monitor** and resolve issues on production.

3. **Spread and integration of DevOps:** More frequent usage of the term "DevSecOps," reflects the intentional and much early inclusion of security aspect in the software development lifecycle. DevOps is also expected to expand into areas such as database teams, QA, and even outside of IT also.

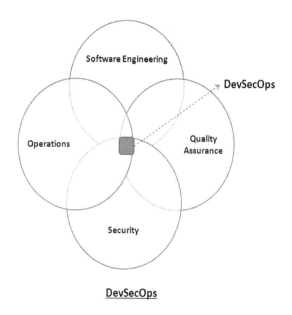

DevSecOps

4. **Increase in ROI**: As we move ahead in the DevOps way of application development IT teams would be more efficient and methodologies, processes, containers and micro services would contribute into higher ROI."The Holy Grail was to be moving faster, accomplishing more and becoming flexible. As these components find broader adoption and organizations become more vested in their

application the results shall appear," says Eric Schabell, global technology evangelist director, Red Hat.

5. **Evolution of success metrics:** On the path to DevOps evolution few points regarding the performance measurement matrices have been realized:
   ✓ Too many metrics to be avoided
   ✓ DevOps metrics should point out what's most important to you
   ✓ Business outcome relationship of the metrics are the key to standardization

Few of the DevOps metrics that may be relevant for the organization may be:

   ✓ Customer ticket volume
   ✓ % of successful deployment
   ✓ Job satisfaction of the deployment team
   ✓ % increase in time for innovation or adding new features

Overall, it is expected that all stakeholder would come together including security and database teams. The frictions caused by these teams would propel the number of releases exponentially.

10. DevOps Success Stories

Amazon is probably the most recognizable DevOps success story because simply put, it's one of the biggest and most recognizable companies in the world. Prior to implementing DevOps, Amazon was still running on dedicated servers. That practice made it very challenging to predict the amount of equipment they need to procure just to be able to meet website traffic demands. In an effort to minimize risks of being unable to meet those demands, Amazon had to pad their equipment requirement estimates just to have leeway for unusual or unexpected spikes in website traffic, which led to excess server capacity, i.e., server capacity wastage of up to 40%. And during shopping seasons like Christmas, up to 75% of server capacity was left unutilized. Economically, that was a very bad proposition.

Amazon's DevOps journey started when it transitioned to the AWS or Amazon Web Services Cloud. This allowed Amazon's engineers to incrementally scale capacity up or down as the need arose and let to substantial reductions in server capacity expenses. It also allowed Amazon to continuously deploy code –

DevOps nirvana – to servers that needed new code whenever they want to.

Within 12 months from moving to AWS, Amazon's engineers were able to deploy code every 12 seconds or less on average. By switching to an Agile approach, Amazon was able to bring down significantly both the frequency and duration of website outages, which in turn increased its revenues.

Another very popular DevOps success story is **Wal-Mart** – the undisputed king of American big-box retail. While it's the undisputed king in physical shopping, it always lagged and struggled behind Amazon. In an effort to cut Amazon's lead and gain much needed online ground, the company put together a very good team by acquiring several tech firms en route to establishing its own technology and innovation arm in 2011, WalmartLabs.

Through WalmartLabs, the parent company purposefully took a DevOps approach to establishing a powerful online presence. The technology and innovation subsidiary incorporated a cloud-based technology called OneOps, which automated and hastened the deployment of apps. Also, it came up with a couple of open source tools like Hapi, which is a Node.js framework that's used to build services and apps that in turn allowed the company's software developers to putting much of their effort and attention on programming multiple-use application logic. In turn, such application logic reduced the amount of time needed for building infrastructure.

By implementing DevOps, Wal-Mart was able to follow in the heels of Amazon.com and has substantially increased its revenues by foraging into the online market segment.

The most popular company that has successfully implemented DevOps is **Facebook.** The social media site practically changed the way the software industry thought about software development. Much of the initial principles it subscribed to in the beginning – including continuous improvements, automation, incremental changes, and code ownership – were considered to be DevOps by nature. Over the years, Facebook's approach has evolved, which has hastened its development lifecycle. In turn, the faster cycle continues to change the way people think about software. By being able to continuously deliver new updates to its app, Facebook continues to make people's experience in the social media platform even more fun, entertaining, and even addictive. It just gets better and better. And in doing so, Facebook was able to grow its business by leaps and bounds to the point where it became one of the biggest publicly listed companies in the New York Stock Exchange, the world's biggest stock market by capitalization. Below are the few latest examples of successful DevOps implementation:

Capital One's DevOps Success: Capital One is one of the largest digital bank in the world and it has been around for 20 years now. Capital One made a shift by adopting DevOps methodology to cater to growing requirements of Digital Banking Services. The approach changed when the engineers instead of writing codes for software and handing it to production team for testing ,fixing and pushing it to production worked together to complete the process using micro services and containers. They utilized the AWS cloud for running applications so that the IT team could focus on building digital products of highest quality.

Their team also insists the inclusion of databases in the DevOps adoption framework. This adoption makes databases respond much quickly to any change and saves time and provides return on investment.

American Airlines DevOps Success: After the acquisition of US Airways in 2013, the two IT teams decided to adopt DevOps as their answer their integration and roadmap issues. It became an opportunity to drive a cultural change at the organization. The two teams working in tandem led to creation of new applications and improved coordinated working culture.

Adobe's DevOps Success: When the organization moved from packaged software to cloud model, it was required to make series of small software updates rather than traditional annual releases. This led to adoption of DevOps methodology to meet the required pace of automating and managing the deployments. This move resulted in better and faster delivery and product management.

Netflix DevOps Success: Since Netflix entered into uncharted territory of streamlining videos instead of shipping DVD's, it required disruptive technologies to sustain its business. Today, the rate at which Netflix has adopted and implemented new technologies through DevOps approach is setting new bars in IT.

Major Success Stories

11. Conclusion

Thank you for buying this book. I hope that through this, you've become familiar with DevOps and Continuous Delivery and how they can help you grow your business. But as the saying goes, knowing is only half the battle and, in this case, the battle for growing your business. The other half is action. As such, I highly recommend that you act on the general knowledge you've gained about DevOps and CD through this book by reading more advanced material on the topic.

I would really appreciate if you can leave your review/feedback on Amazon.

Here's to DevOps and Continuous Delivery for your business success my friend. Cheers!

Stephen Fleming

My Other Books available across the platforms in e-book, paperback and audible versions:

1. Blockchain Technology : Introduction to Blockchain Technology and its impact on Business Ecosystem

2. Love Yourself: 21 day plan for learning "Self-Love" to cultivate self-worth ,self-belief, self-confidence & happiness

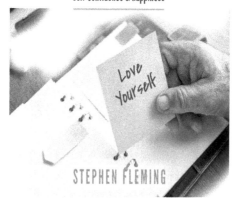

3. Intermittent Fasting: 7 effective techniques of Intermittent Fasting

7 EFFECTIVE TECHNIQUES OF
INTERMITTENT FASTING
Stay Healthy,Lose Weight,
Slow Down Aging Process & Live Longer!

STEPHEN FLEMING

DevOps

HANDBOOK

Introduction to DevOps and its
impact on Business Ecosystem

STEPHEN FLEMING

❖ **DevOps Handbook:
Introduction to DevOps
and its impact on
Business Ecosystem**

Here Is a Preview of what you'll learn...

- What is DevOps

- Relationship between Agile, Scrum, Kanban and DevOps

- DevOps Adoption: Organizational cultural Change

- DevOps Ecosystem

- Emerging Trends

- DevOps success stories

In the **Bonus Booklet** you will find out:

✓ DevOps Job Market overview
✓ Insights into DevOps job application
✓ People to follow on social media for updated news/development

✓

** If you prefer audible versions of these books, I have few free coupons, drop me a mail at: valueadd2life@gmail.com. If available, I would mail you the same.

Book 2: Microservices Architecture Handbook

Non-Programmer's Guide for Building Microservices

119

reparation, damages, or monetary loss due to the information herein, either directly or indirectly.

Respective authors own all copyrights not held by the publisher.

The information herein is offered for informational purposes solely, and is universal as so. The presentation of the information is without contract or any type of guarantee assurance.

The trademarks that are used are without any consent, and the publication of the trademark is without permission or backing by the trademark owner. All trademarks and brands within this book are for clarifying purposes only and are the owned by the owners themselves, not affiliated with this document.

BONUS MICROSERVICES BOOKLET

Dear Friend,

I am privileged to have you onboard. You have shown faith in me and I would like to reciprocate it by offering the maximum value with an amazing gift. I have been researching on the topic and have an excellent "Microservices Booklet" for you to take your own expedition on the subject to next level.

- Do you want to know the best online courses to begin exploring the topic?
- Do you want to know major success stories of Microservices implementation?
- What are the latest trends and news?

Also, do you want once in a while updates on interesting implementation of latest Technology; especially those impacting lives of common people? "Get Instant Access to Free Booklet and Future Updates"

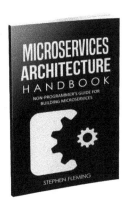

Type Link:
http://eepurl.com/ds8sfD

or

QR Code : You can download a QR code reader app on your mobile and open the link by scnning below:

1. Introduction

As the disruption of technologies continues to play a role in our lives, the application development process is becoming more flexible and agile. You must have heard about the concepts of Agile, DevOps, Kanban and many more. All these terminologies are basically making the application of development or the program writing exercise more flexible, more independent, and faster.

The Microservices architecture develops an application as a collection of loosely coupled services which is meant for different business requirements. Therefore, this architecture supports the continuous delivery/deployment of large, complex applications. It also enables the organization to evolve its application development capabilities.

Who can use this book?

This book can be used by a beginner, Technology Consultant, Business Consultant and Project Manager who are not directly into coding. The structure of the book is such that it answers the most asked questions about Microservices. It also covers the best and the latest case studies with benefits. Therefore, it is expected that after going through this book, you can discuss the topic with any stakeholder and take your agenda ahead as per your role. Additionally, if you are new to the industry, and looking for an application development job, this book will help you to prepare with all the relevant information and understanding of the topic.

2. Monolith and Microservices

Microservices

In May 2011, a workshop of software architects was held in Venice and coined the term "Microservices" to relate to an upcoming software architectural technique that many of the software architectures had been researching. It wasn't until May 2012that Microservices was approved to be the most appropriate term to describe a style of software development. The first case study relating to Microservices architecture was presented by James Lewis in March, 2012, at the 33rd Degree in Krakow in Microservices-Java the Unix way. To date, numerous presentations about Microservices have been made at various conferences worldwide, with software architects presenting different designs and software components of Microservices and its integration to different platforms and interfaces, such as Microsoft architecture and URI interface. Currently, Microservices has grown incredibly and has become an ideal way of developing small business applications, thanks to its efficiency and scalability. This software development technique is particularly perfect for developing software or applications compatible with a range of devices, both developed and yet to be developed, and platforms.

Microservices Defined

A standard definition of Microservices is not yet available, but it can be described as a technique of software application development which entails developing a single application as a suite of independently deployable, small, modular service. Every service controls processes and communicates with each other through a well-defined, lightweight mechanism, often as HTTP resource API to serve a business goal. Microservices are built around business capabilities and are independently deployable by a fully automated deployment mechanism. They can be written in different programming languages such, as Java and C++ and employ different data storage technologies to be effective in the central management of enterprises or small businesses.

Microservices communicate to one other in several ways based on the requirements of the application employed in its development. Many developers use HTTP/REST with JSON or Protobuf for efficient communication. To choose the most suitable communication protocol, you must be a DevOps professional, and in most situations, REST (Representation State Transfer) communication protocol is preferred due to its lower complexity compared to other protocols.

Monolith Defined

A monolith is a software application whose modules cannot be executed independently. Thismakes monoliths difficult to use in distributed systems without specific frameworks or ad hoc solutions, such as Network Objects, RMI or CORBA. However, even these approaches still endure the general issues that affect monoliths, as discussed below.

Problems of Monoliths

1. Large-size monoliths are hard to maintain and evolve due to their complexity. Finding bugs requires long perusals through their code base.

2. Monoliths also suffer from the "dependency hell," in which adding or updating libraries results in inconsistent systems that either do not compile/run or, worse, misbehave.

3. Any change in one module of a monolith requires rebooting the whole application. For large projects, restarting usually entails considerable downtimes, hindering the development, testing, and

maintenance of the project.

4. Deployment of monolithic applications is usually suboptimal due to conflicting requirements on the constituent models' resources: some can be memory-intensive, others computational-intensive and others require ad hoc components (e.g. SQL-based, rather than graph-based databases). When choosing a deployment environment, the developer must compromise with a one-size-fits-all configuration, which is either expensive or suboptimal with respect to the individual modules.

5. Monoliths limit scalability. The usual strategy for handling increments of inbound requests is to create new instances of the same application and to split the load amongst said instances. Moreover, it could be the increased traffic stresses only a subset of the modules, making the allocation of the newer resources for the other components inconvenient.

6. Monoliths also represent a technology lock-in for developers, which are bound to use the same language and frameworks of the original application

7. The Microservices architectural style has been proposed to cope with such problems as discussed above.

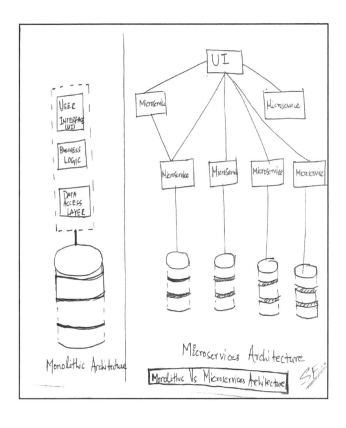

User Interface (UI)

Business Logic

Data Access Layer

Monolithic Architecture

UI

Microservice

Microservice

Microservice

Microservice

Microservice

Microservice

Microservices Architecture

Monolithic Vs Microservices Architecture

Future of Microservices

Over the years, software application development has evolved from Service-Oriented Architecture (SOA) to monolith architecture and now microservices architecture, which is the most preferred software application technique. Global organizations such as Amazon, eBay, Twitter, PayPal, The Guardian, and many others have not only migrated but also embraced microservices over SOA and Monolith architectures in developing their websites and applications. Will Microservices be the future of software application development? Time will tell.

Microservices compared to SOA

Microservices vs. SOA has generated lots of debate amongst software application developers, with some arguing that microservices is simply a refined improved version of SOA, while others consider microservices as a whole new concept in software application development which does not relate in any way with SOA. Nonetheless, microservices have a lot of similarities to SOA. The main difference between SOA and microservices may be thought to lie in the size and scope as suggested by the term "micro, "meaning small. Therefore, microservices are significantly smaller compared to SOA, and are deployed as an independent single unit. Furthermore, an SOA entails either numerous microservices or a single monolith. This debate can be concluded by referring to SOA as a relative of microservices. Nevertheless, they all perform the same role of software programme development, albeit in different ways.

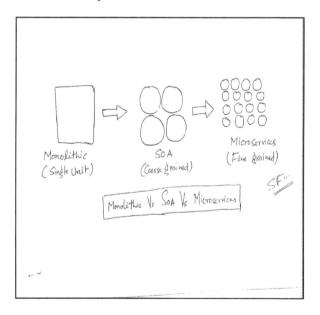

Features of Microservices Architecture

The features of microservices architecture differs widely as not all microservices have the same properties. However, we have managed to come up with several features that may be deemed appropriate and repetitive in almost all microservices.

Independent Deployment

Microservices are autonomous and can be deployed separately, making them less likely to cause system failures. This is done using components, which are defined as a unit of software that is independently replaceable and upgradeable. In addition to components, microservices architecture utilizes libraries or services. Libraries are components attached to a program using in-memory function calls. On the other hand, services are out-of-process components that communicate through different mechanisms, such as web service request mechanism Microservices applications. Software componentization involves breaking them into miniature components, termed as services. A good microservices architecture uses services as components rather than libraries, since they are independently deployable. An application consisting of multiple libraries cannot be deployed separately in a single process, since a single change to any component results in development and deployment of the entire application. An application consisting of multiple services is flexible and only a service is redeployed, rather than the entire application from a change in numerous service changes. It is therefore advantageous over library components.

Decentralized Data Management

This is a common feature in most Microsystems and involves the centralization of conceptual models and data storage decisions. This feature has been praised by small business enterprises, since a single database stores data from essentially all applications. Furthermore, each service manages its own database through a technique called Polyglot Persistence. Decentralization of data is also key in managing data updates in microservices systems. This guarantees consistency when updating multiple resources. Microservices architecture requires transactionless coordination between services to ensure consistency, since distributed transactions may be difficult to implement. Inconsistency in data decentralization is prevented through compensating operations. However, this may be difficult to manage. Nonetheless, inconsistency in data decentralization should be present for a business to respond effectively to real-time demand for their products or services. The cost of fixing inconsistencies is less compared to loss in a business experiencing great consistency in their data management systems.

Decentralized Governance

The microservices key feature is decentralized governance. The term governance means to control how people and solutions function to achieve organizational objectives. In SOA, governance guides the development of reusable service, developing and designing services, and establishing agreements between service providers and consumers. In microservices, architecture governance has the following capabilities;

- There is no need for central design governance, since microservices can make their own decisions concerning its design and implementation

- Decentralized governance enables microservices to share common and reusable services

- Some of the run-time governance aspects, such as SLAs, throttling, security monitoring and service discovery, may be implemented at the API-GW level, which we are going to discuss later

Service Registry and Service Discovery

Microservices architecture entails

dealing with numerous microservices, which dynamically change in location owing to their rapid development/deployment nature. Therefore, to find their location during a runtime, service registry and discovery are essential.

Service registry holds the microservices instance and their location. Microservices instance is registered with the service registry on start-up and deregistered on shutdown. Clients can, therefore, find available services and their location through a service location

Service discovery is also used to find the location of an available service. It uses two mechanisms, i.e. Client-Side Discovery and Service-Side Discovery

Advantages of Microservices

Microservices comes with numerous advantages, as discussed below:

Cost effective to scale

You don't need to invest a lot to make the entire application scalable. In terms of a shopping cart, we could simply load balance the product search module and the order-processing module while leaving out less frequently used operation services, such as inventory management, order cancellation, and delivery confirmation.

Clear code boundaries

This action should match an organization's departmental hierarchies. With different departments sponsoring product development in large enterprises, this can be a huge advantage.

Easier code changes

The code is done in a way that it is not dependent on the code of other modules and is only achieving isolated functionality. If it is done right, the chances of a change in microservices affecting other microservices are very minimal.

Easy deployment

Since the entire application is more like a group of ecosystems that are isolated from each other, deployment could be done one microservices at a time, if required. Failure in any one of these would not bring the entire system down.

Technology adaptation

You could port a single microservices or a whole bunch of them overnight to a different technology without your users even knowing about it. And yes, hopefully, you don't expect us to tell you that you need to maintain those service contracts, though.

Distributed system

This comes as implied, but a word of caution is necessary here. Make sure that your asynchronous calls are used well, and synchronous ones are not really blocking the whole flow of information. Use data partitioning well. We will come to this a little later, so don't worry for now.

Quick market response

The world being competitive is a definite advantage; otherwise, users tend to quickly lose interest if you are slow to respond to new feature requests or adoption of a new technology within your system.

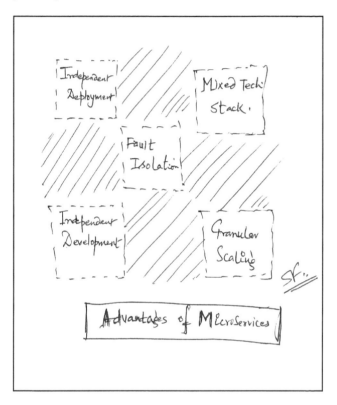

3. Understanding Microservices Architecture

Microservices have different methods of performing their functions based on their architectural style, as a standard microservices model does not exist. To understand microservices architecture, we should first analyze it in terms of service, which can be described as the basic unit in microservices. As briefly defined in chapter 1, Services are processes that communicate over a network to fulfill a goal using technology-agnostic protocols such as HTTP. Apart from technologic-agnostic protocols as a means of communication over a network, services also utilize other means of inter-process communication mechanisms, such as a shared memory for efficient communication over networks. Software developed through microservices architecture technique can be broken down into multiple component services. Each of the components in a service can be deployed, twisted according to the developer's specifications and then independently redeployed without having to develop an entirely new software application. However, this technique has its disadvantages, such as expensive remote calls, and complex procedures when redeploying and redistributing responsibilities between service components.

Services in microservices are organized around business capabilities such as user interface, front-end, recommendation, logistics, billing etc. The services in microservices can be implemented using different programming languages, databases, hardware, and software environments, depending on the developer's preferences. Microservices utilizes the cross-functional team, unlike a traditional monolith development approach where each team has a specific focus on technology layers, databases, Uls, server-side logic or technology layers. Each team in microservices is required to implement specific products based on one or more individual service communicating via a message bus. This improves the communicability of microservices over a network between a business enterprise and the end users of their products. While most software development technique focuses on handing a piece of code to the client and in turn maintained by a team, microservices employs the use of a team who owns a product for a lifetime.

A microservices based architecture adheres to principles such as fine-grained interface, business-driven development, IDEAL cloud application architectures, polyglot programming and lightweight container deployment and DevOps with holistic service monitoring to independently deploy services. To better our understanding of microservices, we can relate it to the classic UNIX system, i.e. they receive a user request, process them, and generate a response based on the query generated. Information flows in a microsystem through the dump pipes after being processed by smart endpoints.

Microservices entails numerous platforms and technologies to effectively execute their function. Microservices developers prefer to use decentralized governance over centralized governance, as it provides them with developing tools which can be used by other developers to solve emerging problems in software application development. Unlike microservices, monoliths systems utilize a single logical database across different platforms with each service managing its unique database.

The good thing about microservices is that it's a dynamic evolutionary software application technique in software application development. Therefore, it's an evolutionary design system which is ideal for the development of timeless applications which is compatible through future technologically sophisticated devices. In summary, Microservices functions by using services to componentized software applications, thereby ensuring efficient communication between applications and users over a network to fulfill an intended goal. The services are fine-grained and the protocols lightweight to break applications into small services to improve modularity and enable users to easily understand the functionality, development, and testing of the application software.

How Microservices Architecture Functions

Just like in programming, microservices have a wide range of functionality depending on the developer's choice. Microservices architecture functions by structuring applications into components or libraries of loosely coupled services, which are fine-grained and the protocols lightweight. But to understand its functionality, we should first look at Conway's law.

Conway's Law

A computer programmer named Melvin Conway came up a law in 1967 which states that "organizations which design system...are constrained to produce designs which are copies of the communication structure of these organization". This means that for a software module to function effectively there should be frequent communication between the authors. Social boundaries within an organization are reflected through the software interface structure within the application. Conway's law is the basic principle of the functionality of microservices and highlights the dangers of trying to enforce an application design that does not match the organizational requirements. To understand this, let's use an example: an organization having two departments i.e. accounting and customer support departments, whose application system are obviously interconnected. A problem arises that the accounting is overworked and cannot handle numerous tasks of processing both dissatisfied customer refunds and credit their accounts while the customer support department is underworked and very idle. How can the organization solve this problem? This is where microservices architecture comes in! The roles and responsibilities of each department in the interconnected system are split accordingly to improve customer satisfaction and minimize business losses in the organization.

In splitting the roles and responsibilities of each department, Interface Separation Principle is essential when implementing microservices to solve this problem. A typical approach isolating issues of concern in an organization through microservices is to find a communication point in the software application, then link the application by drawing a "dotted line" between the two halves of the system. However, this technique, if not carefully carried out, leads to smaller growing monoliths, which leads to isolation of important codes on the wrong side of the barrier.

Avoiding Monoliths in Microservices architecture application

Accidental monoliths are common problems when developing software applications using microservices architecture. An application may become infected with unhealthy interdependencies when service boundaries are blurred, and one service can start using the data source interface of another or even for code related to a certain logic or function to be spread over multiple places due to accidental monoliths which grow with time. This can be avoided by establishing the edge of developed application software graph.

Key Points in the Working of Microservices Architecture

- Its programming of the modern era, where we are expected to follow the SOLID principles. It's object-oriented programming (OOP).

- It is the best way to expose the functionality of other or external components in a way that any other programming language will be able to use the functionality without adhering to any specific user interfaces, that is, services (web services, APIs, rest services, and so on).

- The whole system works

according to a type of collaboration that is not interconnected or interdependent.

- Every component is liable for its own responsibilities. In other words, components are responsible for only one functionality.

- It segregates code with a separation concept, and the segregated code is reusable.

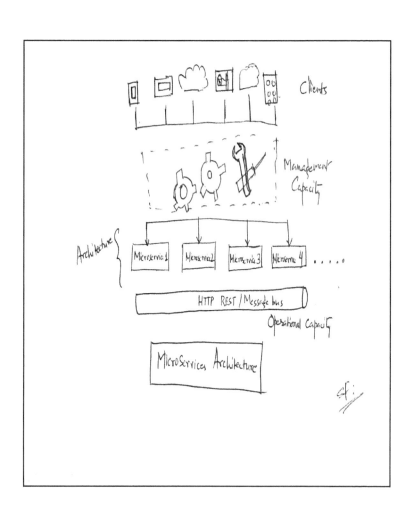

Clients

Management
Capacity

Architecture

| Microservice 1 | Microservice 2 | Microservice 3 | Microservice 4 | . . . . .

HTTP REST / Message bus

Operational Capacity

MicroServices Architecture

152

4. Building Microservices

We have introduced and described the functionality of microservices. In this chapter, we are going to discuss how to build microservices by separating them from the existing system and creating separate services for products and orders which can be deployed independently. First, we will begin by discussing the core concepts, programming languages, and tools that can be used to build microservices.

C#

In 2002, Microsoft developed the C# programming language and the latest release is the C# 7.0. C# is an object-oriented language and component oriented, with features like Deconstructors, ValueTuple, pattern matching, and much more.

Java Programming Language

Java is a general-purpose programming language that is concurrent, class-based, object-oriented and designed to have few implementation dependencies as possible to let application developers "write once, run anywhere" (WORA), meaning that it can run on all platforms that support Java.

Entity Framework Core

Entity framework core is a cross-platform version of Microsoft Entity Framework and can be used as a tool to build microservices. It is one of the most popular object-relational mappers (ORMs). ORM can be defined as a technique to query and manipulate data as per required business output.

.Net Framework

Developed by Microsoft, .NetFramework is a software framework that runs on Microsoft Windows with Framework Class Library to provide language interoperability across several programming languages. Programs are written for .NET Framework execute software environment, rather than hardware environment, or Common Language Runtime(CLR)

Visual Studio 2017

Visual Studio 2017 is an Integrated Development Environments (IDE) developed by Microsoft to enable software application developers to build applications using various programming languages, such as Java, C#, and many more.

Microsoft SQL Server

Microsoft SQL Server(MSSQL) is a software application that has a relational database software management system which is used to store and retrieve data as requested by other software applications. It can be used in the management of microservices and it is able to communicate across a network.

Aspects of Building Microservices

To build microservices, we should first look at the important aspects, such as size and services to ensure their effective functionality after separating them from the main system.

Size of microservices

In building microservices, the first step is to break or decompose applications or systems into smaller segments or functionalities of the main application known as services. Factors to consider for high-level isolation of microservices are discussed below.

Risk due to requirement changes

It is important to note that a change in one microservice should be independent of the other microservices. Therefore, software should be isolated into smaller components termed as services in a way that if there are any requirement changes in one service, they will be independent from other microservices.

Changes in Functionality

In building microservices, we isolate functionalities that are rarely changed from the dependent functionalities that can be frequently modified. For example, in our application, the customer module notification functionality will rarely change. But its related modules, such as Order, are more likely to have frequent business changes as part of their life cycle.

Team changes

We should also consider isolating modules in such a way that one team can work independently of all the other teams. If the process of making a new developer productive—regarding the tasks in such modules—is not dependent on people outside the team, it means we are well placed.

Technology changes

Technology use needs to be isolated vertically within each module. A module should not be dependent on a technology or component from another module. We should strictly isolate the modules developed in different technologies, or stacks, or look at moving them to a common platform as the last resort.

In building microservices, the primary goal is to isolate services from the main application system and keep it as small as possible.

Features of a good Service

A good service is essential in the buildingof a good microservices architecture. A good service that can be easily used and maintained by developers and users should have the following characteristics.

Standard Data Formats

A good service should follow standardized data formats, while exchanging services or systems with other components. Most popular data formats used in the.Netstack are XML and JSON

Standard communication protocol

Good services should adhere to standard communication formats such as SOAP and REST.

Loose coupling

Coupling refers to the degree of direct knowledge that one service has of another. Therefore, loosely coupled means that they should not have little knowledge of the other service, so that a change in one service will not impact the other service.

Domain -Driven Design in building Microservices

Domain-Driven Design (DDD) is a technique in designing complex systems and can be useful in designing and building microservices. DDD can be described as a blueprint used to build microservices and, once it's done, a microservices can implement it just the way an application implements, let's say, an order service or an inventory service. The main principle in domain design is to draft a model which can be written in any programming language after understanding an exact domain problem. A domain driven model, should be reusable, loosely coupled, independently designed, and should be easily isolated from a software application without having to deploy a new system.

After building microservices from a domain-based model. It is important to ensure that the size of the microservices is small enough. This can be done by having a baseline for the maximum number of domain objects which can communicate to each other. You can also do this by verifying the size all interfaces and classes in each microservices. Another way of ensuring a small size of microservices is by achieving the correct vertical isolation of services. You can then deploy each of the services independently. By deploying each service independently, we allow the host in an application to perform its independent process which is beneficial in harnessing the power of the cloud and other hybrid models of hosting.

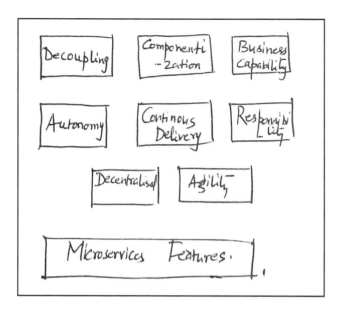

Building Microservices from Monolithic Application

As discussed earlier, the functionality in microservices lies in the isolation of services from the rest of application system translating into advantages discussed in *chapter 1*such as code reusability, independent deployment and easier code maintenance. Building microservices from monolithic application needs thorough planning. Many software architects have different approaches when it comes to transiting from monoliths to microservices, but the most important thing to consider is a correct method, as there is a possibility microservices failing to carry out their function when translated from monolith application using a wrong method. Some of the factors to consider when building microservices from the monolithic application are discussed below:

Module interdependency

When building microservices from the monolithic application, the starting point should always be to identify and pick up those parts of the monolithic application that are least dependent on other modules and have the least dependent on them. This part of the application is essential in identifying isolating application codes from the rest of the system, thereby becoming a part of the microservices which are then deployed independently in the final stage of the process. This small part of the application is referred as seams.

Technology

Technology in the form of an application's base framework is important in achieving this process. Before choosing a software framework, such as the ones discussed in this chapter, you should first identify their features. Building microservices is heavily dependent on data structures, inter-process communication being performed, and the activity of report generation. In this regard, a developer should therefore choose a framework that has great features and is ahead in technology, as they enable them to perform the transition correctly

Team structure

Team structure is important in the transition, as they are the workforce in building microservices. Teams greatly differ based on the geographical location, security of the company, and their technical skills. For the team to optimize their productivity in building microservices, they should be able to work independently. Furthermore, the team should safeguard the intellectual property of the company in developing a microservices based application.

Database

The database is considered the biggest asset of a system and their domain is defined by database tables and stored procedure. Contrary to most misconceptions, building microservices from the monolithic application does not involve dividing the whole database at once, but rather a step-by-step procedure. First, a database structure used to interact with the database is identified. Then the database structure is isolated into separate codes, which are then aligned with the newly defined vertical boundaries. Secondly, the underlying database structure is broken using the same method as the first step. The database change should not define the module used in the transition to microservices-style architecture, but rather the module should define the database. The database structure should relate to the modules picked in the transition to ensure ease in building microservices.

It is important to understand the types of acceptable changes in breaking down and merging a database, as not all changes can be implemented by the system due to data integrity. When restructuring a database to match the microservices architecture, removing foreign key relationship is the most important step, as microservices are designed to function independently of other services in an application. The final step in breaking database in microservices-style architecture is isolating the ORDER table from the ProductID, as they are still sharing information, i.e. loose coupling.

In summary, breaking down a database in microservices architecture style involves two important steps: Isolating the data structures in the code and removing foreign key relationships. It is important to note that splitting the database is not the final step in building microservices from monolithic applications, as there are other steps.

Transaction

After splitting the database from the steps mentioned above, the next step is to link services to the database in a way that ensures data integrity is maintained. However, not all services successfully go through a transaction to their successful databases due to several reasons, such as a communication fault within the system or insufficient quantities for the product requested in e-commerce platforms. For example, Amazon and e-commerce. These problems can be solved by orchestrating the whole transaction, record individual transactions across the service, or to cancel the entire transaction across the services in the system. However, when the transactions are planned out well in a microservices-style architecture application, this problem can be avoided

Building Microservices with Java

Building microservices in a java ecosystem includes container-less, self-contained and in-container strategies, all of which are discussed below.

166

Container-less microservices

Container-less microservices package the application, with all of its dependencies, into a single JAR file. This approach is very advantageous, due to the ease of starting and stopping services as necessary in scaling. A JAR file is also conveniently passed around by the team members that need it.

Self-contained microservices

Like container-fewer microservices, microservices are packaged into a single fat JAR file with the inclusion of embedded framework with optional compatible third-party libraries, such as Wildfly Swarm and Spring Boot, both of which will be discussed later in this chapter.

In-Container microservices

In-container microservices package an entire Java EE container and its service implementation in a Docker image. The container provides verified implementations through standard APIs, giving the developer the opportunity to solely focus on business functionality.

Microservices Framework for Java

Apart from the containers discussed above, building microservices in Java entails several microservices frameworks, such as Spring Boot, Jersey, Swagger, Dropwizard, Ninja Web Framework, Play Framework, and many more. We are going to handle just a few common microservices frameworks below.

Microservices in Spring Boot

Spring Boot is one of the best microservices frameworks, since it is optimally integrated with supporting languages. You can Spring Boot on your own device via an embedded server. Spring Boot also eliminates the necessity of using Java EE containers.This is enabled through the implementation of Tomcat. Spring boot projects include:

Spring IO Platform: An enterprise-grade distribution for versioned applications.

Spring Framework: Used for

transaction management, data access, dependency injection, messaging, and web apps.

Spring Cloud: Used for distributed systems and also used for building or deploying your microservices.

Spring Data: Used for microservices that are related to data access, be it map-reduce, relational or even non-relational.

Spring Batch: Used for higher levels of batch operations.

Spring Security: Used for authorization and authentication support.

Spring REST Docs: Used for documenting RESTful services.

Spring Social: Used for connecting to social media APIs.

Spring Mobile: Used for mobile Web apps.

Microservices in Dropwizard

Dropwizard combines mature and stable

Java libraries in lightweight packages for use in a certain application. It uses Jetty for HTTP, Jersey for REST, and Jackson for JSON, along with Metrics, Guava, Logback, Hibernate Validator, Apache HTTP Client, Liquibase, Mustache, Joda Time, and Freemarker. Maven is used to set up Dropbox application, after which a configuration class, an application class, a representation class, a resource class, or a health check can be created to run the applications.

Jersey

Jersey is an open source framework based on JAX-RS specifications. Jersey's applications can extend existing JAX-RS implementations with more features and utilities to make RESTful services and client development simpler and easier. Jersey is fast and easily routed, coupled with great documentation filled with examples for easy practice.

Play Framework

Play Framework provides an easier way to build, create, and deploy Web

170

applications using Scala and Java. It is ideal for REST application that requires parallel handling of remote calls. It is one of the most used microservices frameworks with modular, and supports async. An example of code in Play Framework is shown below.

Restlet

Restlet enables developers to create fast and scalable WEB APIs that adhere to the RESTful architecture pattern discussed above. It has good routing and filtering, and it's available for Java SE/EE, OSGi, Google AppEngine, Android, and other major platforms. However, learning Restlet can be difficult due to the small number of users and the unavailability of tutorials. An example of a code in Restlet is shown below.

5. Integrating Microservices

Integrating microservices refers to interaction and communication of independent services located in a separate database within a software application. First, let us look at communication between microservices.

Communication between Microservices

Microservices communicate using an inter-process communication mechanism with two main message formats, namely binary and text. There are two kinds of inter-process communication mechanisms that microservices can be used to communicate, i.e. asynchronous messaging and synchronous request/response, both of which are discussed below.

Asynchronous Communication

This is an inter-process communication

mechanism in which microservices communicate by asynchronously exchanging messages. It means that when an organizational client sends a message to a service to perform a certain task or answer a query, the service replies by sending a separate message back to the client. The messages, consisting of a title and body, are exchanged over channels with no limitation to the number of organizations and their clients sending and receiving messages. Likewise, any number of consumers can receive multiple messages from a single communication channel. There are two types of channels, namely: publish-subscribe and point-to-point channels. A point-to-point channel delivers a message to exactly one client reading from the channel, while the publish-subscribe channel delivers a common message to all the attached clients in a certain organization. Services utilize point-to-point channel to communicate directly to clients and publish-subscribe communication to interact with one too many clients attached to an organization

For instance, when a client requests a trip through an application, The Trip Management is notified and in turn notifies the Dispatch department about the new trip through a Trip Created message to a publish-subscribe channel. The Dispatcher then locates an available driver and notifies them by writing a Driver Proposed message to a publish-subscribe channel.

Some of the advantages of this type of communication include message buffering, isolating the client from the service, flexibility in client-service interactions, and explicitly in inter-process communication. However, there are certain downsides, such as additional operational costs, since the system is a separate entity and must be installed, configured, and operated separately, and the complexity of implementing request/ response-based interaction.

Synchronous, Request/Response IPC Mechanism

In this inter-process mechanism, a client

sends a request to a service, which in turn processes the request and sends back a response. The client believes that the response will arrive in a timely fashion. While using synchronous IPC mechanism, one can choose various protocols to choose from, but the most common ones are REST and Thrift, as discussed below.

REST
REST is an IPC mechanism that uses HTTP to communicate. The basic in REST is a resource which can be equated to a business entity, such as a product or a customer or a collection of business objects. REST utilizes HTTP verbs referenced using a URL to manipulate resources. The key benefit of using this protocol is that it's simple and familiar and supports request/response-style communication, thereby enabling real-time communication within an organization and numerous clients. Some of the drawbacks include that the intermediary and buffer messages must all run concurrently and that the client must know the location of each service through a URL.

Thrift

An alternative to REST is the Apache Thrift, which provides a C-style IDL for defining APIs. Thrift is essential in generating client-side stubs and server-side skeletons. A thrift interface is made up of one or more services, which can return a value to implement the request/response style of interaction. Thrift also supports various message formats such, as JSON, binary, and compact binary.

Integration Patterns

We have discussed communication between microservices through synchronous and asynchronous inter-process communication, but this alone does not guarantee integration, as integration patterns are also essential in their communication. We will discuss the implementation of various integration patterns required by an application.

The API Gateway

The API gatewaysits between clients and services by acting as a reverse proxy, routing requests from clients to services. It acts as a proxy between services and client applications. The Azure API management as an example is responsible for the following functionalities.

- Accepting API calls

- Verifying API keys, JWT tokens, and certificates

- Supporting Auth through Azure AD and OAuth 2.0 access token

- Enforcing usage quotas and rate limits

- Caching backend responses

- Logging call metadata for analytics purposes

To understand the integration of microservices in Azure API gateway, let's use an example of an application split into microservices, namely product service, order service, invoice service, and customer service. In this application,the Azure API will be working as an API Gateway to connect clients to services. The API gateway enables clients to access services in servers unknown to them by providing its own server address and authenticating the client's request by using a valid *Ocp-Apim-Subscription-Key*

Different API commands execute certain functions in a service, as shown in the table below:

API Resource	Description
GET /api/product	Gets a list of products
GET /api/product/{id}	Gets a product
PUT /api/product/{id}	Updates an existing product
DELETE /api/product/{id}	Deletes an existing

	product
POST /api/product	Adds a new product

The Event-Driven pattern

A microservice has a database per service pattern, meaning that it has an independent database for every dependent or independent service. Dependent services require a few external services or components, and internal services to function effectively. Dependent service does not work if any or all the services on which the service is dependent on do not work properly. Independent service does not require any other service to work properly, as the name suggests.

In the diagram, the event-manager could be a program which runs on a service which enables it to manage all the events of the subscribers. Whenever a specific event is triggered in the Publisher, the event-manager notifies a Subscriber.

Event Sourcing

Event sourcing pattern enables developers to publish an event whenever the state changes. The EventStore persists the events available for subscription, or as other services. In this pattern, tasks are simplified to avoid additional requirements in synchronizing the data model and business domain, thereby improving responsiveness, scalability, and responsiveness in the microservices. For example, in an application having ORDERSERVICE as the services, a command issues a book for the User Interface to be ordered. ORDERSERVICE queries and populates the results with the `CreateOrder` event from the Event Store. The command handler raises an event to order the book, initiating a related operation. Finally, the system authorizes the event by appending the event to the event store.

Compensating Transactions

Compensating transactions refers to a means used to undo tasks performed in

180

a series of steps. For instance, a service has implemented operations in a series and one or more tasks have failed. Compensating transactions is used to reverse the steps in a series.

Competing Consumers

Competing consumers is essential in processing messages for multiple concurrent consumers to receive the messages on the same channel. It enables an application to handle numerous requests from clients. It is implemented by passing a messaging system to another service through asynchronous communication.

Azure Service Bus

Azure Service Bus is an information delivery service used to enhance communication between two or more services. Azure Service Bus can be described as a means through which services communicate or exchange information. Azure Service Bus provides two main types of service, which are broken and non-broken communication. Broken communication is a real-time communication that ensures communication between a sender or a receiver, even when they are offline. In non-broken communication, the sender is not informed whether information has been received or not by the receiver.

Azure queues

Azure queues are cloud storage accounts which use Azure Table. They provide a means to queue a message between applications.

In summary, integrating microservices is through communication between services. Microservices communicate through inter-service communication, which can be synchronous or asynchronous. In asynchronous inter-process communication, API gateway is used to allow clients to communicate to services by acting as an intermediary between clients and services. Microservices also communicate through various patterns, as discussed in the chapter.

6. Testing Microservices

Testing microservices is an important way of ensuring their functionality by assessing the system, applications, or programs in different aspects to identify an erroneous code. Testing microservices varies in systems, depending on the microservices architectural style employed.

How to Test Microservices

It is easier to test a monolithic application than to test microservices, since monoliths provide implementation dependencies and short note delivery cycles. This is because testing microservices involves testing each service separately, with the test technique different for each service. Testing microservices can be challenging, since each service is designed to work independently. Therefore, they are tested individually rather than as a whole system It gets more challenging when testing is combined with continuous integration and deployment. However, these challenges can be solved by using a unit test framework. For example, Microsoft Unit Testing Framework, which provides a facility to test individual operations of independent components. These tests are run on every compilation of the code to ensure success in the test.

Testing Approach

As mentioned above, different application systems require different testing approaches. The testing strategy should be unique to a system and should be clear to everyone, including the none technical members of a team. Testing can be manual or automated and should be simple to perform by a system user. Testing approaches have the following techniques.

Proactive Testing

A testing approach that tries to fix defects before a build is created from the initial test designs

Reactive Testing

Testing is started after the completion of

coding.

Testing Pyramid

To illustrate testing microservices, we use the testing pyramid. The Testing pyramid showcases how a well-designed test strategy is structured.

Testing Pyramid:

- System Tests (Top)

- Service Tests (Middle)

- Unit Tests (Bottom)

Unit Test

Unit testing involves testing small functionalities of an application based on the microservices architectural style.

Service Tests

Service tests entail testing an independent service which communicates with another/external service

System Tests

They are end-to-end tests, useful in

185

testing the entire system with an aspect of the user interface. System testsare expensive and slow to maintain and write, while service and unit testsare fast and less expensive.

Types of Microservices Test

There are various types of microservices test, as discussed below.

Unit Testing

Unit testing is used to test a single function in a service, thereby ensuring that the smallest piece of the program is tested. They are carried out to a verify a specific functionality in a system without having to test other components in the process. Unit testing is very complex, since the components are broken down into independent, small components that can be tested independently. A Test-Driven Development is used to perform a unit test.

Component (service) Testing

In service testing, the units(UI) are directly bypassed and the API, such as

.Net Core Web API, is tested directly. Testing a service involves testing an independent service or a service interacting with an external device. A mock and stub approach is used to test a service interacting with an external service through an API gateway.

Integration Testing

Integration testing involves testing services in components working together. It is meant to ensure that the system is working together correctly as expected. For example, an application has StockService and OrderService depending on each other. Using integration testing, StockService is tested individually by ensuring it does not communicate with OrderService. This is accomplished through mock.

Contract Testing

Contract testing is a test that involves verifying response in each independent service. In this test, any service that is dependent on an external service is stubbed, therefore making it function independently. This test is essential in checking the contract of external services through consumer-driven contract, as discussed below.

Consumer-driven contracts

Consumer-driven refers to an integration pattern, which specifies and verifies interactions between clients and the application through the API gateway. It specifies the type of interactions a client is requesting with a defined format. The applications can then approve the requests through consumer-driven contract.

Performance Testing

It is a non-functional testing with the aim of ensuring the system is performing perfectly according to its features, such as scalability and reliability. Performance testing involves various techniques, as described below.

Load Testing

This technique involves testing the behavior of the application system under various conditions of a specific load, such as database load, critical transactions, and application servers

Stress Testing

It is a test where the system is exposed to regress stressing to find the upper capacity of the system. It is aimed at determining the behavior of a system in critical conditions, such as when the current load overrides the maximum load.

Soak Testing

Also called endurance testing, soak testing is aimed at monitoring memory utilization, memory leaks, and other factors influencing system performance

Spike Testing

Spike testing is an approach inwhich the system is tested to ensure it can sustain the workload. It can be done by suddenly increasing the workload and monitoring system performance

End-to-end (UI/functional) testing

UI test is performed on the whole system, including the entire service and database. This test is the highest level of testing in microservices and it's mainly performed to increase the scope of testing. It includes fronted integration.

Sociable versus isolated unit Tests

Sociable tests resemble system tests and are performed to ensure that the application is running smoothly and as expected. Additionally, it tests other software in the same application environment. Isolated software, on the other hand, is performed before stubbing and mocking to perform unit testing, as discussed earlier. Unit testing can also be used to perform using stubs in concrete class

Stubs and Mocks

Stubs and mocks are the mockimplementations of objects interacting with the code when performing a test. The object can be replaced with a stub in one test and a mock on the other, depending on the intention of the test. Stubs can be referred to as inputs to the code under test, while mocks are outputs of a code under test

Summary

We have discussed that testing microservices is more challenging compared to testing monolithic applications in a .Net framework. The pyramid test concept enables us to understand and strategize the testing procedures. Unit test is used in testing small functionalities and class in a microservices application. Tests on top of the pyramid, such as end-end testing, are used to test the entire microservices application, rather than small functionalities or services in the application.

7. Deploying Microservices

Deploying microservices can also be challenging and is done through continuous integration and continuous deployment. Additionally, new technology such as toolchain technology and container technologies have proven essential in deploying microservices. In this chapter, we are going to discuss the basics of microservices deployment and the new technologies mentioned above. But first let's look at the key requirements in their deployment.

Deployment Requirement

- Ability to deploy/un-deploy services independent of other microservices

- A service must be able to, at each microservices level, ensure a given service does not receive more traffic compared to other services in the application.

- A failure in one microservices must not affect other services in the application

- Building and deploying microservices quickly

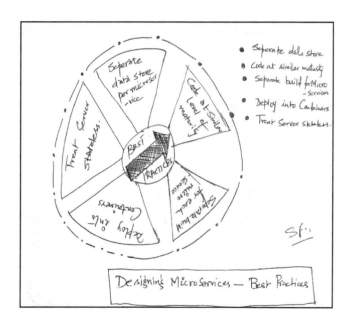

Designing Microservices — Best Practices

Steps in Microservices Deployment

In this section, we are going to discuss the first step, i.e. Build to the final stage, which is the release stage.

Build Stage

In the build stage, a docker container is made to provide the necessary tools to create the microservices. A second container is then applied to run the built container. Then, a service source is compiled carefully to prevent errors. The services are later tested using unit testing to ensure their correspondence. The final product in this stage is a build artifact.

Continuous Integration (CI)

Any changes in the microservices build the entire application through CI. This occurs because the application code gets compiled and a comprehensive set of automated tests are run against it. CI was developed due to the problem of frequent integration. The basic idea behind CI is to ensure small changes in the software application by preserving a Delta.

Deployment

Requirements for deployment include the hardware specifications, base OS, and the correct version of a software framework. The final part is to promote the build artifacts produced in the first stage. In microservices, there is a distinction between the deployment stage and the release stage.

Continuous Deployment (CD)

In this stage, each build is deployed to the production. It is important in the deployment of microservices, as it ensures that the changes pushed to production through various lower environment work as expected in the production. This stage involves several practices, such as automated unit testing, labeling, versioning of build numbers, and traceability of changes.

Continuous Delivery

Continuous delivery is different from continuous deployment(CD) and it's focused on providing the deployment code as early as possible to the customer. In Continuous Delivery, every build is passed through quality checks to prevent errors. Continuous Delivery is implemented through automation by the build and deployment pipeline. Build and deployment pipelines ensure that a code is committed in the source repository.

Release

This is the final stage in microservices deployment and involves making a service available to possible clients. The relevant build artifact is deployed before the release of a service managed by a toggle.

Fundamentals for Successful Microservices Deployment

For microservices to be deployed successfully, the following things should be done.

Self-sufficient Teams

A team should have sufficient members

with all the necessary skills and roles i.e. developers and analysts. A self-sufficient team will be able to handle development, operations, and management of microservices effectively. Smaller self-sufficient teams, who can integrate their work frequently, are precursors to the success of microservices.

CI and CD

CI and CD are essential in implementing microservices, as they automate the system to be able to push code upgrades regularly, thereby enabling the team to handle complexity by deploying microservices, as discussed above.

Infrastructure Coding

Infrastructure coding refers to representing hardware and infrastructure components, such as network servers into codes. It is important to provide deployment environments to make integration, testing, and build production possible in microservices production. It also enables developers to produce defects in lower environments. Tools such as CFEngine, Chef, Puppet, Ansible and PowerShell DSC can be used to code infrastructure. Through infrastructure coding, an infrastructure can be put under a version control system, then deployed as an artifact to enhance microservices deployment.

Utilization of Cloud Computing

Cloud computing is important in the adoption and deployment of microservices. It comes with near infinite scale, elasticity, and rapid provision capability. Therefore, it should be utilized to ensure successful deployment of microservices.

Deploying Isolated Microservices

In 2012, Adam Wiggins developed a set of principles known as a 12-factor app, which can be used to deploy microservices. According to the principles, the services are essentially stateless except for the database. These principles are applied in deploying isolated microservices as follows.

Service teams

The team should be self-sufficient and built around services. They should be able to make the right decision to develop and support microservices decision.

Source control isolation

Source control isolation ensures that microservices do not share any source code or files in their respiratory. However, codes can be duplicated to avoid this problem.

Build Stage Isolation

Build and deploy pipelines for microservices should be isolated and separate. For isolated deployed services, build and deploy pipelines run separately. Due to this, the CI-CD tool is scaled to support different services and pipelines at a faster stage.

Release Stage Isolation

Every microservice is released in isolation with other services.

Deploy Stage Isolation

It is the most important stage in deploying isolated microservices.

Containers

Containers can be defined as pieces of software in a complete file system. Container technology is new and is now linked to the Linux world. Containers are essential in running code, runtime, system tools, and system libraries. They share their host operating system and kernel with other containers on the same host.

Deploying Microservices with Docker.

Docker is an open-source engine that lets developers and system administrators deploy self-sufficient application containers (defined above) in Linux environment. It is a great way to deploy microservices. The building deploying when starting microservices is much faster when using the Docker platform. Deploying microservices using docker is performed by following these simple steps.

- The microservices is packaged as a Docker container image

- Each service is deployed as a container

- Scaling is done based on changing the number of container instances.

Terminologies used in Docker

Docker image

A Docker image is a read-only template containing instructions for creating a Docker container. It consists of a separate filesystem, associated libraries, and so on. It can be composed of layers on top each other, like a layered cake. Docker images used in different containers can be reused, thereby reducing the deployment footprints of applications using the same images. A Docker image can be stored at the Docker hub.

Docker registry

Docker registry is a library of images

and can either be private or public. It can also be on the same server as the Docker daemon or Docker client, or on a totally different server.

Dockerfile

A Dockerfile is a scripted file containing instructions on how to build a Docker image. The instructions are in the form multiple steps, starting from obtaining the base image.

Docker Container

Refers to a runnable instance of a Docker image.

Docker Compose

It enables a developer to define application components i.e. containers, configuration, links, volumes in a single service. A single command is then executed to establish every component in the application and run the application.

Docker Swarm

It's a Docker service in which container nodes function together. It operates as a defined number of instances of a replica task in a Docker image.

Deploying Microservices with Kubernetes

Kubernetes is a recent technology in deploying microservices. It extends Docker capabilities, since Linux containers can be managed in a single system. It also allows the management and running of Docker containers across multiple hosts offering co-location of containers, service discovery, and replication control. Kubernetes has become an extremely powerful approach in deploying microservices, especially for large-scale microservices deployments.

Summary

We have discussed that for microservices to be deployed effectively, developers should adhere to the best deployment practices, as discussed in this chapter. Containers are effective in microservices deployment as they isolate services. Microservices can be deployed using either Docker or Kubernetes, as discussed above,

8. Security in Microservices

Securing microservices is a requirement for an enterprise running their applications or websites on microservices, since data breaches or hacking are very common these days and can lead to massive unwarranted loses. As much as security in an organization is everyone's responsibility, microservices should be secured after their deployment, as we are going to discuss in this chapter. First, let's look at security in monolithic applications.

Security in Monolithic Applications

As we discussed earlier, monolithic applications are deployed dependently, thereby they have a large surface area in an application compared to microservices. The fact that microservices are isolated from each other and deployed independently means that they are more secure, compared to monoliths. However, implementing security in microservices

205

can be challenging. The monolithic application has different attack vectors from microservices, and their security is implemented as follows.

- Security in a typical monolithic application is about finding 'who is the intruder' and 'what can they do' and how do we propagate the information.

- After establishing this information, security is then implemented from a common security component which is at the beginning of the request handling chain. The component uses an underlying user respiratory or a store to populate the required information.

This is done through an authentication (auth) mechanism, which verifies the identity of a user and manages what they can or cannot access through permissions. Data from client to the server is then secured through encryption achieved through HTTPS protocol. In a.Net monolithic application, a user files a request to a web application through a web browser which requires them to enter their username and password. This request is then transferred through HTTPS and load balancer to the Auth, which then connects to the user credential store container, such as SQL server, which contains login details of various users. The user-supplied credentials i.e. username and password, are then verified against the ones retrieved from credentials store by the auth layer.

On verification, the user's browser automatically creates a cookie session, enabling him or her to access the requested information. In this kind of monolithic application, security is achieved by ensuring that the application modules do not separate verification and validation of request while communicating with each other.

Security in Microservices

Security in microservices architecture is achieved by translating the pattern used in securing monolithic applications to microservices. In microservices, the authentication layer is broken into microservices in different applications, which will need its authentication mechanisms. The user credential store is different for every microservices. From our previous discussion, this pattern cannot be implemented, since auth cannot be synced across all devices, and validating inter-process communication might be impossible. Additionally, modern applications based on Android or iOS cannot support secure information between clients and services, since session-based authentication using cookies is not possible, as in monolithic applications.So, the question is how these problems are solved to secure microservices application. The solution comes in the form of OpenID Connect, JSON Web Tokens and OAuth 2.0, as we will discuss below.

JSON Web Tokens

JSON Web Tokens(JWT) is used in producing a data structure which contains information about the issuer and the recipient, along with the sender's identity. They can be deployed independently, irrespective of OAuth 2.0 or OPENID Connect, as they are not tied together. The tokens are secured with symmetric and asymmetric keys to ensure information received by a client is authentic or trustable.

The OAuth 2.0

The OAuth 2.0 is an authorization framework that lets a third-party application to obtain finite access to a HTTP service, either on behalf of the resource owner by orchestrating an approval interaction between the resource owner and the HTTP service, or by allowing the third-party application to obtain access on its behalf. OAuth 2.0 functions as a delegated authorization framework, relying on authentication mechanisms to complete authorization framework. The figure below illustrates the functionality of OAuth in securing microservices.

OpenID Connect

It comes top of OAuth 2.0 protocol and

its importance in the user authentication i.e. standard for authentication. It allows a client to verify end users based on the authentication performed by an authorization server. It is also used to obtainthe basic profile information of end users. Clients using any device, i.e. web-based, mobile and javascript can access information relating to authenticated sessions and end users through OpenID Connect. Validation of the end user is through sending ID token to an application used by a client.

To understand microservices security, let's use an example of a client requesting a service through his/ her mobile-based microservices application. OAuth and the OpenID Connect (Authorization Server)authenticates the client to access data in the microservices by issuing the Access Token. The API Gateway is the only entry to the application's microservices, then receives the Access Token along with the client's request. The Token Translation at the API Gateway extracts the Access token from the client's request and sends it to the authorization server to retrieve the JSON Web Tokens. JSON tokens, along with the client's request, are then passed to the microservices layer by the API Gateway. JSON Web Token contains the necessary information used in storing user sessions. At each microservices layer, there are components used to process the JSON tokens, thereby obtaining the client's request and its information.

Other Security Practices

There are other practices to secure microservices apart from OAuth 2.0 and Open ID connect, as we are going to discuss below.

Standardization of libraries and frameworks

This refers to introducing libraries and frameworks in the development process. It is done to ease out patching, in case of any vulnerability found. It also minimizes the risk introduced by ad hoc implementation of libraries or tools around development.

Regular vulnerability Identification and mitigation

The vulnerability is regularly checked using an industry-standard vulnerability scanner to scan the source code, coupled with binaries and the findings addressed accordingly.

Third-party audits and penetration testing.

External audits and penetration test are conducted regularly as they are essential in ensuring data integrity in applications or websites involving sensitive critical data or information

Logging and monitoring

Logging is useful in detecting and recovering from hacking attacks by aggregating logs from different systems and services, thereby essential in microservices security.

Network Segregation

Network segregation or partitioning,

although only possible in the monolithicapplication, can be effective in ensuring the security of microservices. This can be achieved through the creation of different network segments and subnets.

Summary

We have discussed that securing microservices is essential to any organization having microservices application systems. Security patterns in a monolithic application cannot be implemented in microservices application due to incompatibility problems, such as each microservices requiring their own authentication mechanism and so on, as discussed in this chapter. Therefore, secure token-based approaches such as OAuth 2.0 and OpenID Connect can be used to secure microservices through authorization and authentication.

9. Criticism and Case Study

The emergence of microservices as a technique in software application development has been largely criticized for some reasons, namely:

- Information barriers due to services

- Communication of services over a network is costly in terms of network latency and message processing time

- Complexity in testing and deployment

- Difficulty in moving responsibilities between services. It involves communication between different teams, rewriting the functionality in another language or fitting it into a different infrastructure.

- Too many services, if not deployed correctly, may slow system performance.

- Additional complexity, such as network latency, message formats, load balancing and fault tolerance.

Nano service

Nano service refers to anti-patterns where a service is too fine-grained, meaning that the overheads outweighs its utility. Microservices have continually been criticized as a Nano service due to numerous problems such as the code overhead, runtime overhead, and fragmented logic. However, there are some proposed alternatives to the Nano service. These are:

- Packaging the functionality as software library rather than a service.

- Combining the functionality with other functionalities to produce a more substantial useful service

- Refactoring the system by putting the functionality in other services or redesigning the system altogether.

Design for Failure

Microservices have been criticized as prone to failure compared to monoliths, since they introduce isolated services to the system, which increases the possibility of having a system failure. Some of the reasons that may lead to failure in microservices include network instability and unavailability of the underlying resources. However, there are certain design mechanisms that may ensure an unavailable or unresponsive microservices does not cause the whole application to fail. It ensures that microservices is fault tolerant and swiftly recovers after experiencing a failure. In microservices, it is important to maintain real-time monitoring, since services can fail at any time. The failures should be repaired quickly to be able to restore the services. Let's discuss common ways of avoiding failure in microservices application.

Circuit Breaker

A circuit breaker is a fault monitor component which is configured to each service in the application. The fault monitor then observes service failures, and when they reach a certain threshold, the circuit breaker stops any further requests to the services. This is essential in avoiding unnecessary resource consumption by requesting delay timeouts. It is also important in monitoring the whole system.

Bulkhead

Since microservices applications comprise of numerous services, a failure in one service may affect the functioning of other microservices, or even the entire application. Bulkhead is essential in preventing a failure in one microservices from affecting the whole application, as it isolates different parts of the microservices application

Timeout

Timeout is a pattern mechanism to prevent clients from overwaiting for a response from microservices once they have sent as a request through there devices. Clients configure a time interval in which they are comfortable to wait for increasing efficiency and client satisfaction.

These patterns are configured to the API Gateway, and monitors the response of the microservices once they receive a request. When a service is unresponsive or unavailable, the Timeout mechanism notifies the user to try accessing the microservices another time to avoid overloading the application system and prevent failure in one service from affecting the other microservices. Additionally, the Gateway can be used as the central point to monitor each microservices, thereby informing developers of a failure.

Microservices Disrupting the Fintech Industries

Microservices have greatly disrupted the Fintech industries and other sectors. By breaking down big, complex systems into smaller pieces or services, microservices allow complicated work to be divided and distributed amongst smaller teams, making it easier to develop, test, and deploy. Fintech industries are realizing that they are being disrupted and need to reinvent them to compete against these digital-only businesses. The speed of innovation is dictated by the ability to expose business assets in a digital-friendly manner, and in some instances leverage external assets to provide a more social experience. The core paradigm enabling the use of business assets within mobile or tablet applications is through microservices. For a large majority of enterprises, microservices have become a new business channel to expose key assets, data, or services for consumption by mobile, web, internet of things, and enterprise applications. It can represent monetary benefit by metering usage of API services, and providing different plans (i.e. Gold, Silver Bronze) at various price-points, or simply making them available at no-charge to increase usage and brand promotion through increased marketing.

Companies using Microservices

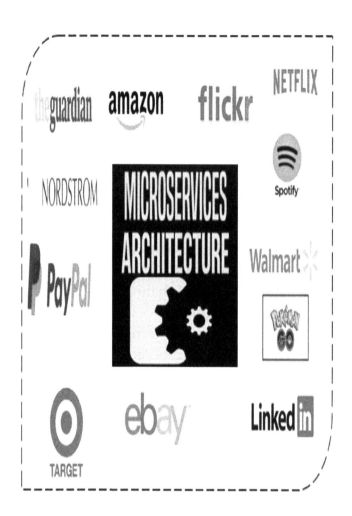

220

10. Summary

We have discussed a lot about microservices from their invention, definition, advantages, building, integration techniques, deployment, and finally their security. In this chapter, we are going to recap what we have already discussed.

Before Microservices?

As we had discussed, before the invention of microservices, monolithic architecture and Service-Oriented Architecture was used to develop software applications

Monolithic Architecture

Monolithic architecture consists of components such as user interface, business logic, and database access, which are interconnected and interdependent. Therefore, a minor change inany module of the application results in a change to the entire application. This would require the redeployment of the entire application. Monolithic architecture has numerous challenges, including code complexity, scalability, large interdependent code, and difficulty in the adoption of a new technology in terms of application or new devices.

Service-oriented architecture

Service-oriented architecture is an improvement of monolithic architecture resolving some of the challenges we mentioned above. Services primarily started with SOA and it's the main concept behind it. As we have already defined, a service is a piece of program or code providing some functionality to the system components. SOA comes with some advantages, such as the ability to reuse codes, and the ability to upgrade applications without necessarily deploying the entire application.

Microservices architecture.

Microservices architecture is very similar to SOA, except that services are deployed independently. A change in a piece of program or code does not change the functionality of the entire application. For services to function independently, a certain discipline and strategy are required. Some of the disadvantages we discussed include clear boundaries, easy deployment, technology adaptation, affordable scalability, and quick market response.

Building Microservices from Monoliths

We discussed building microservices from an existing monolithic application. First is to identify decomposition candidates within a monolith based on parameters including code complexity, technology adaptation, resource requirement, and human dependency. Second is the identification of seams, which act as boundaries in microservices, then the separation can start. Seams should be picked on the right parameters depending on module interdependency, team structure, database. and existing technology. The master database should be handled with care through a separate service or configuration. An advantage of microservices having its own database is that it removes many of the existing foreign key relationships, thereby has a high transaction-handling ability.

Integration Techniques

Microservices integration techniques are mainly based on communication between microservices. We discussed that there are two ways in which microservices communicate: synchronous and asynchronous communication. Synchronous communication is based on request/response, while asynchronous style is event-based. Integration patterns are essential to facilitate complex interaction among microservices. We discussed integrating microservices using event-driven patterns in the API Gateway. The event-driven pattern works by some services publishing their events, and some subscribing to those available events. The subscribing services simply react independently to the event-publishing services, based on the event and its metadata.

Deployment.

We discussed microservices deployment and how it can be challenging for various reasons. Breaking the central database further increases the overall challenges. Microservices deployment requires continuous delivery(CD) and continuous integration (CI) right from the initial stages. Infrastructure can be represented with codes for easy deployment using tools such as CFEngine, Chef, Puppet, and PowerShell DSC. Microservices can be deployed using Docker or Kubernetes after containerization.

Testing microservices

We discussed the test pyramid representing the types of test. Unit test is used to verify small functionalities in the entire application, while system test is used to verify the entire application on its functionality. The mock and stub approach is used in microservices testing. This approach makes testing independent of other microservices and eliminates challenges in testing the application's database due to mock database interactions. Integration testing is concerned with external microservices communicating with them in the process. This is done through mocking external services.

Security

Securing microservices is essential to an organization to ensure data integrity. In a monolithic application, security is attained through having a single point of authentication and authorization. However, this approach is not possible in microservices architecture, since each service needs to be secured independently. Therefore, the OAuth 2.0 authorization framework, coupled with OpenID Connect, is used to secure microservices. OAuth 2.0's main role is to authorize clients into the application system as we discussed in *chapter 7*. One provider of OAuth 2.0 and OpenID Connect is the Azure Active Directory (Azure AD)

Conclusive Remarks

It is our hope that this book has been essential in your understanding of the microservices architecture by answering all your questions based on this wide subject. Microservices architecture is a pretty new concept, and is still in development. Therefore, the contents of this book may change overtime.

My Other Books available across the platforms in e-book, paperback and audible versions:

1. **Blockchain Technology : Introduction to Blockchain Technology and its impact on Business Ecosystem**

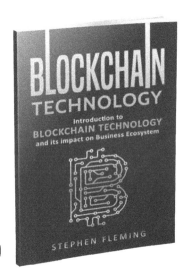

2. DevOps Handbook: Introduction to DevOps and its Impact on Business Ecosystem

3. Blockchain Technology and DevOps : Introduction and Impact on Business Ecosystem

4. **Love Yourself: 21 day plan for learning "Self-Love" to cultivate self-worth ,self-belief, self-confidence & happiness**

5. **Intermittent Fasting: 7 effective techniques of Intermittent Fasting**

7 EFFECTIVE TECHNIQUES OF
INTERMITTENT FASTING

**Stay Healthy,Lose Weight,
Slow Down Aging Process & Live Longer!**

STEPHEN FLEMING

6. Love Yourself and intermittent Fasting(Mind and Body Bundle Book)

You can check all my Books on my **Amazon's Author Page**

** If you prefer audible versions of these books, I have few free coupons, mail me at valueadd2life@gmail.com. If available, I would mail you the same.

Book3:
Kubernetes
Handbook

A Non-Programmer's Guide

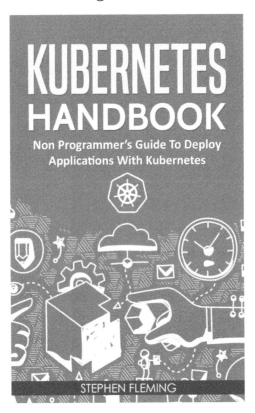

BONUS TECHNOLOGY BOOKLET

Dear Friend,
I am privileged to have you onboard. You have shown faith in me and I would like to reciprocate it by offering the maximum value with an amazing booklet which contains latest technology updates on DevOps and Blockchain.

"Get Instant Access to Free Booklet and Future Updates"

- Link: http://eepurl.com/dge23r

OR

- QR Code : You can download a QR code reader app on your mobile and open the link:

1. Preface

This book has been well written as a guide to *getting started with Kubernetes, how they operate and how they are deployed*.

The book also explains the features and functions of Kubernetes and how it can be integrated into a total operational strategy for any project.

Additionally, the reader will be able to learn how to deploy real-world applications with Kubernetes.

The book has been written in a simple, easy to comprehend language and can be used by Non-Programmers, Project Managers, Business Consultants or any other persons with an interest in Kubernetes.

2. Introduction

Kubernetes Defined

Kubernetes, also known as K8s is an open-source container-orchestration system that can be used for programming deployment, scaling, and management of containerized applications. Kubernetes were innovated with the aim of providing a way of automatically deploying, scaling and running operations of container applications across a wide range of hosts. A container is a standalone, lightweight and executable package of a part of the software that is composed of components required to run it, i.e., system tools, code, runtime, system libraries, and settings. Containers function to segregate software from its adjacentenvironment, i.e., for instance, variances in development and staging environments thereby enabling the reduction of conflicts arising when teams run separate software on the same network infrastructure.

Containers may be flexible and really fast, attributed to their lightweight feature, but they are prone to one problem: they have a short lifespan and are fragile. To overcome this enormous problem and increase the stability of the whole system, developers utilize Kubernetes to schedule and orchestrate container systems instead of constructing each small component, making up a container system bullet-proof. With Kubernetes, a container is easily altered and re-deployed when misbehaving or not functioning as required.

Kubernetes Background

The initial development of Kubernetes can be attributed to engineers working in industries facing analogous scaling problems. They started experimenting with smaller units of deployment utilizing cgroups and kernel namespaces to develop a process of individual deployment. With time, they developed containers which faced limitations, such that they were fragile, leading to a short lifetime; therefore, Google came up with an innovation calling it Kubernetes, a Greek name meaning "pilot" or "helmsman" in an effort aimed at sharing their own infrastructure and technology advantage with the community at large. The earliest founders were Joe Beda, Brendan Burns and Craig McLuckie who were later joined by Tim Hockin and Brian Grant from Google. In mid-2014, Google announced the development of Kubernetes based on its Borg System, unveiling a wheel with seven spokes as its logo which each wheel spoke representing a nod to the project's code name. Google released Kubernetes v1.0, the first version of their development on July 21, 2015, announcing that they had partnered with Linux Foundation to launch the Cloud Native Computing Foundation (CNCF) to promote further innovation and development of the Kubernetes. Currently, Kubernetes provides organizations with a way of effectively dealing with some of the main management and operational concerns faced in almost all organizations worldwide, by offering a solution for administration and managing several containers deployed at scale, eliminating the practice of just working with Docker on a manually-configured host.

Advantages Of KUBERNETES

While Kubernetes was innovated to offer an efficient way of working with containers on Google systems, it has a wider range of functionalities and can be used essentially by anyone regardless of whether they are using the Google Compute Engine on Android devices. They offer a wide range of advantages, with one of them being the combination of various tools for container deployments, such as orchestration, services discovery and load balancing. Kubernetes promotes interaction between developers, providing a platform for an exchange of ideas for the development of better versions. Additionally, Kubernetes enables the easy discovery of bugs in containers due to its beta version.

3. How Kubernetes Operates

Kubernetes design features a set of components referred to as primitives which jointly function to provide a mechanism of deploying, maintaining and scaling applications. The components are loosely coupled with the ability to be extensible to meet a variety of workloads. Extensibility is attributed to the Kubernetes API, which is utilized by internal components coupled with extensions and containers that operates on Kubernetes. In simple, understandable terms, Kubernetes is basically an object store interacting with various codes. Each object has three main components: the metadata, a specification and a current status that can be observed; therefore, a user is required to provide metadata with a specification describing the anticipated state of the objects. Kubernetes will then function to implement the request by reporting on the progress under the

243

status key of the object.

The Kubernetes architecture is composed of various pieces which work together as an interconnected package. Each component at play has a specified role, some of which are discussed below. Additionally, some components are placed in the container/cloud space.

- *Master*- It is the overall managing component which runs one or more minions.

- *Minion* –Operatesunder the master to accomplish the delegated task.

- *Pod*- A piece of application responsible for running a minion. It is also the basic unit of manipulation in Kubernetes.

- *Replication Controller*- Tasked with confirming that the requested number of pods are running on minions every time.

- *Label*- Refers to a key used by the Replication Controller for service discovery.

- **Kubecfg**- A command line used to configure tools.

- **Service**- Denotes an endpoint providing load balancing across a replicated group of pods.

With these components, Kubernetes operate by generating a master which discloses the Kubernetes API, in turn, allowing a user to request the accomplishment of a certain task. The master then issues containers to perform the requested task. Apart from running a Docker, each node is responsible for running the Kubelet service whose main function is to operate the container manifest and proxy service. Each of the components is discussed in detail in this chapter.

Docker and Kubernetes

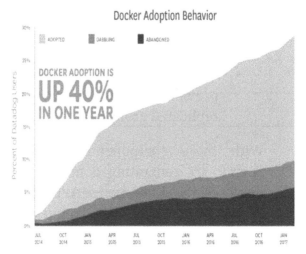

Docker Adoption Behavior

DOCKER ADOPTION IS
UP 40%
IN ONE YEAR

While Docker and Kubernetes may appear similar and help users run applications within containers, they are very different and operate at different layers of the stack, and can even be used together. A Docker is an open source package of tools that help you "Build, Ship, and Run" any app anywhere, and also enables you to develop and create software with containers. The use of a Docker involves the creation of a particular file known as a Dockerfile which defines a build process and

246

produces a Docker image when the build process is integrated to the 'Docker build' command. Additionally, Docker offers a cloud-based repository known as the Docker Hub which can be used to store and allocate the created container images. Think of it like GitHub for Docker Images. One limitation involved in the use of Docker is that a lot of work is involved in running multiple containers across multiple devices when using microservices. For instance, the process involves running the right containers at the right time; therefore, you have to work out how the containers will communicate with each other, figure out storage deliberations and handle or redeploy failed containers or hardware. All this work could be a nightmare, especially when you are doing it manually; therefore, the need for Kubernetes.

Unlike Docker, Kubernetes is an open-source container orchestration platform which allows lots of containers to harmoniously function together automatically, rather than integrating every container separately across multiple machines, thus cutting down the operational cost involved. Kubernetes has a wide range of functions, some of which are outlined below:

- Integrating containers across different machines.

- Redeploying containers on different machines in case of system failure.

- Scaling up or down based on demand changes by adding or removing containers.

- They are essential in maintaining the consistent storage of multiple instances of an application.

- Important for distributing load between containers.

As much as Kubernetes is known for container management, Docker also can manage containers using its own native container management tool known as Docker Swarm, which enables you to independently deploy containers as

Swarms which then interact as a single unit. It is worth noting that Kubernetes interacts only with the Docker engine itself and never with Docker Swarm.

As mentioned above, Kubernetes can be integrated with the Docker engine with an intention of co-ordinating the development and execution of Docker containers on Kubelet. In this type of integration, the Docker engine is tasked with running the actual container image built by running 'Docker build.' Kubernetes, additionally, handles higher level concepts, including service-discovery, load balancing, and network policies.

Interestingly, as much as Docker and Kubernetes are essentially different from their core, they can be used concurrently to efficiently develop modern cloud architecture by facilitating the management and deployment of containers in the distributed architecture.

Containers are the new packaging format because they're efficient and portable

- App Engine supports Docker containers as a custom runtime
- Google Container Registry: private container image hosting on GCS with various CI/CD integrations
- Compute Engine supports containers, including managed instance groups with Docker containers
- The most powerful choice is a container **orchestrator**

Pods: Running Containers in Kubernetes

Pods area group of containers and volumes which share the same resource - usually an IP address or a filesystem, therefore allowing them to be scheduled together. Basically, a pod denotes one or more containers that can be controlled as a single application. A pod can be described as the most basic unit of an application that can be used directly with Kubernetes and consists of containers that function in close association by sharing a lifecycle and should always be scheduled on the same node. Coupled containers condensed in a pod are managed completely as a single unit and share various components such as the environment, volumes and IP space.

Generally, pods are made into two classes of containers: a main container which functions to achieve the specified purpose of the workload and some helper containers which can optionally be used to accomplish closely-related tasks. Pods are tightly tied to the main application, however, some applications may benefit by being run and managed in their containers. For instance, a pod may consist of one container running the primary application server and a helper container extracting files to the shared file system, making an external repository detect the changes. Therefore, on the pod level, horizontal scaling is generally discouraged as there are other higher level tolls best suited for the task.

It is important to note that Kubernetes schedules and orchestrates functionalities at the pod level rather than the container level; therefore, containers running in the same pod have to be managed together in a concept known as the shared fate which is key in the underpinning of any clustering system. Also, note that pods lack durability since the master scheduler may expel a pod from its host by deleting the pod and creating a new copy or bringing in a new node.

Kubernetes assigns pods a shared IP enabling them to communicate with each other through a component called a localhost address, contrary to Docker configuration where each pod is assigned a specific IP address.

Users are advised against managing pods by themselves as they do not offer some key features needed in an application, such as advanced lifecycle management and scaling. Users are instead invigorated to work with advanced level objects which use pods or work with pod templates as base components to implement additional functionality.

Replication and Other Controllers

Before we discuss replication controllers and other controllers, it is important to understand Kubernetes replication and its uses. To begin with, being a container management tool, Kubernetes was intended to orchestrate multiple containers and replication. Replication refers to creating multiple versions of an application or container for various reasons, including enhancing reliability, load balancing, and scaling. Replication is necessary for various situations, such as in microservices-based applications to provide specific functionality, to implement native cloud applications and to develop mobile applications. Replication controllers, replica sets, and deployments are the forms of replications and are discussed below:

Replication Controller

A replication controller is an object that describes a pod template and regulates controls to outline identical replicas of a pod horizontally by increasing or decreasing the number of running copies. A Replication controller provides an easier way of distributing load across the containers and increasing availability natively within Kubernetes. This controller knows how to develop new pods using a pod template that closely takes after a pod definition which is rooted in the replication controller configuration.

The replication controller is tasked to ensure that the number of pods deployed in a cluster equals the number of pods in its configuration. Thus, in case of failure in a pod or an underlying host, the controller will create new pods to replace the failed pods. Additionally, a change in the number of replicas in the controller's configuration, the controller will either initiate or kill containers to match the anticipated number. Replication controllers are also tasked to carry out rolling updates to roll over a package of pods to develop a new version, thus minimizing the impact felt due to application unavailability.

Replication Sets

Replication sets are an advancement of replication controller design with greater flexibility with how the controller establishes the pods requiring management. Replication sets have a greater enhanced replica selection capability; however, they cannot perform rolling updates in addition to cycling backends to a new version. Therefore, replication sets can be used instead of higher level units which provide similar functionalities.

Just like pods, replication controllers and replication sets cannot be worked on directly as they lack some of the fine-grained lifecycle management only found in more complex tools.

Deployments

Deployments are meant to replace replication controls and are built with replication sets as the building blocks. Deployments offer a solution to problems associated with the implementation of rolling updates. Deployments are advanced tools designed to simplify the lifecycle of replicated pods. It is easy to modify replication by changing the configuration which will automatically adjust the replica sets, manage transitions between different versions of the same application, and optionally store records of events and reverse capabilities automatically. With these great features, it is certain that deployment will be the most common type of replication tool used in Kubernetes.

Master and Nodes

Initially, minions were called nodes, but their names have since been changed back to minions. In a collection of networked machines common in data centers, one machine hosts the working machines. The working machines are known as nodes. The master machine is responsible for running special co-ordinating software that schedules containers on the nodes. A collection of masters and nodes are known as clusters. Masters and nodes are defined by the software component they run.

The master is tasked to run three main items:

- API Server - The API server ensures that all the components on the master and nodes achieve their respective tasks by making API calls.

- Etcd - This is a service responsible for keeping and replicating the current configuration and run the state of the cluster. It is implemented as a lightweight distributed key-value store.

- Scheduler and Controller Manager- These processes schedule containers, specifically pods, onto target nodes. Additionally, they may correct numbers of the running processes.

A node usually carries out three important processes, which are discussed below:

- Kubelet- It is an advanced

background process (daemon) that runs on each node and functions to respond to commands from the master to create, destroy and monitor containers on that host.

- Proxy - It is a simple network proxy that can be used to separate the IP address of a target container from the name of the services it provides.

- cAdvisor- It is an optional special daemon that collects, aggregates, processes, and exports information about running containers. The information may exclude information on resource isolation, historical usage, and key network statistics.

The main difference between a master and a node is based on the set of the process being undertaken.

The 10,000-foot view

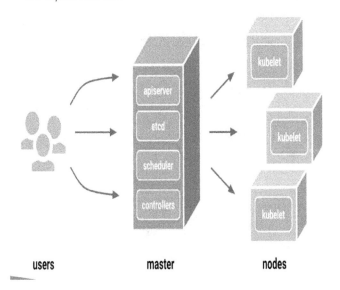

users   master   nodes

Services

A service assigns a fixed IP to your pod replicas and allows other pods or services to communicate with them

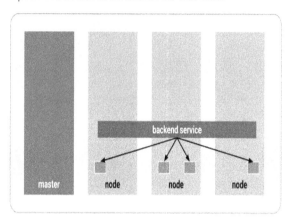

In Kubernetes, a service is an important component that acts a central internal load balancer and representatives of the pods. Services can also be defined as a long-lasting, well-known endpoint that points to a set of pods in a cluster. Services consist of three critical components: an external IP address (known as a portal, or sometimes a portal IP), a port and a label selector. Service is usually revealed through a small proxy process. The service proxy is responsible for deciding which pod to route to an endpoint request via a label

260

selector. It also acts as a thin look-up service to determine a way of handling the request. The service proxy is, therefore, in simple terms, a tuple that maps a portal, port, and label selector.

A service abstraction is essential to allow you to scale out or replace the backend work units as necessary. A service's IP address remains unchanged and stable regardless of the changes to the pods it routes too. When you deploy a service, you are simply gaining discoverability and can simplify your container designs. A service should be configured any time you need to provide access to one or more pods to another application or external consumers. For example, if you have a set of pods running web servers that should be accessible from the internet, a service will provide the necessary concept. Similarly, if a web service needs to store and recover data, an internal service is required to authorize access to the database pods.

In most circumstances, services are only available via the use of an internally routable IP address. However, they can also be made available from their usual places through the use of several strategies, such as the NodePort configuration which works by opening a static port on each node's external networking interface. In this strategy, the traffic to the external port is routed automatically using an internal cluster IP service to the appropriate pods. Instead, the Load Balancer service strategy can be used to create an external load balancer which, in turn, routes to the services using a cloud provider's load balancer integration. The cloud controller manager, in turn, creates an appropriate resource and configures it using an internal service address. In summary, the main functionality of services in Kubernetes is to expose a pod's unique IP address which is usually not exposed outside the cluster without a service.

You can have multiple services with different configurations and features

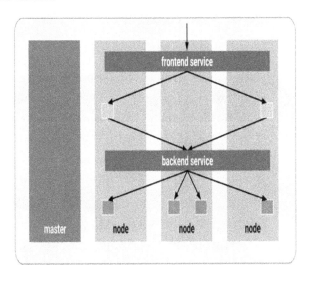

Service Discovery

Service discovery refers to the process of establishing how to connect to a service. Services need dynamically to discover each other to obtain IP addresses and port detail which are essential in communicating with other services in the cluster.Kubernetes offers two mechanisms of service discovery: DNS and environmental variable. While there is a service discovery option based on environmental variables available, most

263

users prefer the DNS-based service discovery. Both are discussed below.

Service Discovery with Environmental Variables

This mechanism of service discovery occurs when a pod exposes a service on a node, initiating Kubernetes to develop a set of environmental variables on the exposed node to describe the new service. This way, other pods on the same node can consume it easily. Managing service discovery using environmental variable mechanism is not scalable, therefore, most people prefer the Cluster DNS to discover services.

Cluster DNS

Cluster DNS enables a pod to discover services in the cluster, thereby enabling services to communicate with each other without having to worry about IP addresses and other fragile schemes. With cluster DNS, you can configure your cluster to schedule a pod and service that expose DNS. Then, when new pods are developed, they are

264

informed of this service and will use it for look-ups. The cluster DNS is made of three special containers listed below:

- Etcd - Important for storing all the actual look-up information.

- SkyDns- It is a special DNS server written to read from etcd.

- Kube2sky - It is a Kubernetes-specific program that watches the master for any changes to the list of services and then publishes the information into etcd. SkyDns will then pick it up.

Apart from environmental variables and cluster DNS, there are other mechanisms which you can use to expose some of the services in your cluster to the rest of the world. This mechanism includes Direct Access, DIY Load Balancing, and Managed Hosting.

Direct Access- Involves configuring the firewall to pass traffic from the outside world to the portal IP of your service. Then, the proxy located on the node selects the container requested by the service. However, direct access faces a problem of limitation where you are constrained to only one pod to service the request, therefore, fault intolerant.

DIY Load Balancing- Involves placing the load balancer in front of the cluster and then populating it with the portal IPs of your service; therefore, you will have multiple pods available for the service request.

Managed Hosting- Most cloud providers supporting Kubernetes offer an easier way to make your services discoverable. All you need to do is to define your service by including a flag named *CreateExternalLoadBalncer* and set its value to *true*. By doing this, the cloud provider automatically adds the portal IPs for your service to a fleet of load balancers that is created on your behalf.

ReplicaSets-Replica Set Theory/Hands-on with ReplicaSets

As mentioned earlier, ReplicaSets is an advanced version of Replication Controller, offering greater flexibility in how the controller establishes the pods it is meant to manage. A ReplicaSet ensures that a specified number of pod replicas are running at any given time. Deployment can be used to effectively manage ReplicaSets as it enables it to provide declarative updates to pods combined with a lot of other useful features.

Using ReplicaSets is quite easy since most Kubernetes commands supporting Replication Controllers also support ReplicaSets except the rolling update command which is best used in Deployments. While ReplicaSets can be used independent of each other, it is best used by Deployments as a mechanism of orchestrating pod creation, deletion, and updates. By using Deployments, you will not have to worry about managing the ReplicaSets they develop as they deploy and manage their ReplicaSets.

Daemon Sets

Daemon Sets are a specialized form of pod controller which runs a copy of a pod on each node in the cluster (or a subset, if specified). Daemon Sets are useful when deploying pods which help perform maintenance and provide services for the nodes themselves by creating pods on each added node, and garbage collects pods when nodes are removed from the cluster. Daemon Sets can be used for running daemons that require running on all nodes of a cluster. Such things can be cluster storage daemons, such as Qubyte, ceph, glusterd, etc., log collectors such as Fluentd or Logstash, or monitoring daemons such as Prometheus Node Exporter, Collectd, New Relic agent, etc.

The daemon can be deployed to all nodes, but it's important to split a single daemon to multiple daemons. Note that in situations involving a cluster with nodes of different hardware requiring adaption in the memory and CPU, you may have to include for the daemon for effective functionality.

There are other cases where you may require different logging, monitoring, or storage solutions on separate nodes of your cluster. In such circumstances where you prefer to deploy the daemons only to a specific set of nodes rather than the entire node, you may use a node selector to specify a subdivision of the nodes linked to the Daemon Set. For this to function effectively, you should have labeled your nodes consequently.

There are four main mechanisms in which you can communicate to the daemons discussed below:

- Push - In this mechanism, the pods are configured to push data to a service, making the services undiscoverable to clients.

- NodeIP and known port - The pods utilize a host port, enabling clients to access each NodeIP via this port.

- DNS - In this mechanism, pods are accessed via a headless service by either the use of an endpoints resource or obtaining several A Records from DNS.

- Service - The pods are accessible via the standard service. The client can access a daemon on a random node using the same service; however, in this mechanism, you may not be able to access a specific node.

Since Daemon Sets are tasked to provide essential services and are required throughout the fleet, they, therefore, are allowed to bypass pod scheduling restrictions which limit other controllers from delegating pods to certain hosts. For instance, attributed to its unique responsibilities, the master server is usually configured to be inaccessible for normal pod scheduling, providing Daemon Sets with the ability to override the limitation on the pod-by-pod basis to ensure that essential services are running.

As per now, Kubernetes does not offer a mechanism of automatically updating a node. Therefore, you can only use the semi-automatic way of updating the pods by deleting the daemon set with the –cascade=false option, so that the pods may allot on the nodes; then you can develop a new Daemon Set with an identical pod selector and an updated pod template. The new Daemon Set will automatically recognize the previous pods, but will not automatically update them; however, you will need to use the new pod templates after manually deleting the previous pods from the nodes.

Jobs

Jobs are workloads used by Kubernetes to offer a more task-built workflow where the running containers are expected to exit successfully after completing the workload. Unlike the characteristic pod which is used to run long-running processes, jobs allow you to manage pods that are required to be terminated rather than being redeployed. A job can create one or more pods and guarantees the termination of a particular number of pods. Jobs can be used to achieve a typical batch-job such as backing up a database or deploying workers that need to function off a specific queue, i.e., image or video converters. There are various types of jobs as discussed below:

Non-parallel Jobs

In this type of job, one pod is usually initiated and goes on to complete the job after it has been terminated successfully. Incase of a failure in the pod, another one is created almost immediately to take its place.

Parallel Job with a fixed completion count

In a parallel job with a fixed completion count, a job is considered complete when there is one successful pod for every value between 1 and the number of completions specified.

Parallel Jobs with a work queue

With parallel jobs with a work queue, no pod is terminated lest the work queue is empty. This means that even if the worker performed its job, the pod could only be terminated successfully when the worker approves that all its fellow workers are also done. Consequently, all other pods are required to be terminated in the process of existing. Requested parallelism can be defined by parallel Jobs. For instance, if a job is set to 0, then the job is fundamentally paused until it is increased. It is worth noting that parallel jobs cannot support situations which require closely-communicating parallel processes, for example, in scientific computations.

CronJobs

CronJobs are used to schedule jobs or program the repetition of jobs at a specific point in time. They are analogous to jobs but with the addition of a schedule in Cron format.

ConfigMaps and Secrets

Kubernetes offers two separate storage locations for storing configuration information: Secrets for storing sensitive information and ConfigMaps for storing general configuration. Secrets and ConfigMaps are very similar in usage and support some use cases. ConfigMaps provides a mechanism of storing configuration in the environment rather than using code. It is important to store an application's configuration in the environment since an application can change configuration through development, staging, production, etc.; therefore, storing configuration in the environment increases portability of applications. ConfigMaps and Secrets are discussed below in detail.

Secrets

As mentioned above, Secrets are important for storing miniature amounts, i.e., less than I MB each of sensitive information such as keys, tokens, and passwords, etc. Kubernetes has a mechanism of creating and using Secrets automatically, for instance, Service Account token for accessing the API from a pod and it is also easy for users to create their passwords. It is quite simple to use passwords; you just have to reference them in a pod and then utilize them as either file at your own specified mount points, or as environmental variables in your pod. Note that each container in your pod is supposed to access the Secret needs to request it explicitly. However, there is no understood mechanism of sharing of Secrets inside the pod.

PullSecrets are a special type of Secret that can be used to bypass a Docker or another container image registry login to the Kubelet so that it can extract a private image for your pod. You need to be extremely cautious when updating Secrets that are in use by running pods since the pods in operation would not automatically pull the updated Secret. Additionally, you will need to explicitly update your pods, i.e., using the rolling update functionality of Deployments discussed above, or by restarting or recreating them. Put in mind that a Secret is namespaced, meaning that they are placed on a specific namespace, and only pods in the same namespace can access the Secret.

Secrets are stored in tmpfs and only stored on nodes that run pods which utilize those Secrets. The tmpfs keep Secrets from being accessible by the rest of the nodes in an application. Secrets are transmitted to and from the API server in plain text; therefore, you have to implement the SSL/TLS protected connections between user and API server and additionally between the API server and kubelets.

To enhance security for secrets, you should encrypt secrets in etcd. To add another layer of security, you should enable Node Authorization in Kubernetes, so that a kubelet can only request Secrets of Pods about its node. This function is to decrease the blast radius of a security breach on a node.

ConfigMaps

ConfigMaps are arguably similar to Secrets, only that they are designed to efficiently support working with strings that do not contain sensitive information. ConfigMaps can be used to store individual properties in the form of key-value pairs; however, the values can also be entirely used to configure files or JSON blobs to store more information. Configuration data can then be used to:

- Configure the environmental variable.

- Command-line arguments for a container.

- Configure files in a volume.

- Storing configuration files for tools like Redis or Prometheus which allows you to change the configuration of containers without having to rebuild the entire container.

ConfigMaps differs from Secrets in that it necessarily gets updated without the need to restart the pods which use them. Nevertheless, depending on how to implement the configuration provided, you may need to reload the configs, e.g., using an API call to Prometheus to reload. This is often done through a sidecar container in the same pod watching for changes in the config file.

The most important thing about ConfigMaps and Secrets is that they function to enhance the versatility of containers by limiting their specificities which allow users to deploy them in different ways. Therefore, users are provided with a choice of reusing containers or among teams, or even outside the organization due to the elimination of container specificity. Secrets are especially helpful when sharing with other teams and organizations, or even when sharing publicly. This enables you to freely share images, for instance, via a public respiratory, without having to worry about any company-specific or sensitive data being published.

How is it going till now? Before moving to the deployment part just recap the topics you just went through. Also, can you spare some time and review the book?

4. Deployments

In Kubernetes, deployments are essential for deploying and managing software; therefore, it is important to comprehend how they function and how to use effectively. Before deployment, there were Replication Controllers, which managed pods and ensured a certain number of them were operating. With deployments, we moved to ReplicaSets, which replaced Replication Controllers later on. ReplicaSets are not usually managed; rather they get managed by Deployments we define through a definite chain, i.e., Deployment-ReplicaSet-Pod(s). In addition to what ReplicaSets offer, Deployment offers you declarative control over the update strategy used for the pods. This replaces the old kubectl rolling-update way of updating, but offers similar flexibility regarding defining maxSurge and maxUnavailable, i.e., how many additional and how many unavailable pods are allowed.

Deployments can manage your updates and even go as far as checking whether or not a new version being rolled out is working, and stop the rollout in case it is not. Additionally, you can indicate a wait time needed by a pod to be ready without any of its containers crashing before it's considered available, prevents "bad updates" giving your containers plenty of time to get ready to handle traffic. Furthermore, Deployments store a history of their revisions which can be used in rollback situations, as well as an event log, that can be used to audit releases and changes to your Deployment.

Integrating Storage Solutions and Kubernetes

Today, organizations are struggling to deliver solutions which will allow them to meet quickly changing business needs, as well as to address competitive pressure. To achieve this, they are utilizing various technologies such as containers, Kubernetes, and programmable infrastructure to achieve continuous integration/continuous development (CI/CD) and DevOps transformations.

For organizations deploying these technologies, they have to ensure tenacious storage across containers as it is important to maximize the number of applications in the model. One such example of an integrated storage solution which can be integrated to Kubernetes is NetApp Trident which is discussed in detail below.

NetApp Trident

Unlike competitive application container orchestration and dynamic storage provisioning plugins, NetApp Trident integrates with Kubernetes' persistent volume (PV) framework. Red Hat OpenShift with Trident provides one interface for dynamic provision of a persistent volume of applications across storage classes. These interfaces can be allocated to any of the storage platforms from NetApp to deliver the optimal storage management capabilities and performance for each application.

Trident was developed as an open source project by NetApp to offer Kubernetes users an external mechanism of monitoring Kubernetes volume and to completely automate the provisioning process. Trident can be integrated to Kubernetes and deployed as a physical server for storage, a virtual host, or a Kubernetes Pod. Trident offers Kubernetes a persistent storage solution and can be used in situations such as:

- In cloud-native applications and microservices.

- Traditional enterprise applications deployed in a hybrid cloud.

- DevOps teams who want to accelerate the CI/CD pipeline.

Trident also provides a boost of advanced features which are designed to offer deployment flexibility in Kubernetes containerized applications, in addition to providing basic persistent volume integration. With Trident, you can:

- Configure storage via a simple Representational State Transfer application programming interface (REST API) with unique concepts that contain specific capabilities to Kubernetes storage classes.

- Protect and manage application data with NetApp enterprise-class storage. Current storage objects, such as volumes and logical unit numbers (LUNs), can easily be used by Trident.

- Based on your choice, you can use separate NetApp storage backends and deploy each with different configurations, thus allowing Trident to provide and consume storage with separate features, and present that storage to container-deployed workloads in a straightforward fashion.

Integrating the Trident dynamic storage provider to Kubernetes as a storage solution offers numerous benefits outlined below:

- Enables you to develop and deploy applications faster with rapid iterative testing.

- It provides a dynamic storage solution across storage classes of the entire storage portfolio of SolidFire, E-Series, NetApp, and ONTAP storage platforms.

- Improves efficiency when developing applications using Kubernetes.

Deploying Real World Application

To give you a better idea on how to deploy the real-world application, we are going to use a real-world application, i.e., Parse.

Parse

Parse is a cloud API designed to provide easy-to-use storage for mobile applications. It offers a variety of different client libraries making it easy to integrate with Android, iOS and other mobile platforms. Here is how you can deploy Parse in Kubernetes:

Fundamentals

Parse utilizes MongoDB cluster for its storage, therefore, you have to set up a replicated MongoDB using Kubernetes StatefulSets. Additionally, you should have a Kubernetes cluster deployed and ensure that the kubectl tool is properly configured.

Building the parse-server

The open source parse-server comes with a Dockerfile for easy containerization of the clone Parse repository.

$ git clone https://github.com/ParsePlatform/parse-server

Then move into that directory and build the image:

$ cd parse-server

$ docker build -t ${DOCKER_USER}/parse-server.

Finally, push that image up to the

Docker hub:

```
$            docker            push
${DOCKER_USER}/parse-server
```

Deploying the parse-server

Once a container image is developed, it is easy to deploy the parse-server into your cluster using the environmental variables configuration below:

APPLICATION-ID-An identifier for authorizing your application.

MASTER-KEY-An identifier that authorizes the master user.

DATABASE-URI-It is the URI for your MongoDB cluster.

When all these are placed together, it is possible to deploy Parse as a Kubernetes Deployment using the YAML as illustrated below:

```yaml
apiVersion: extensions/v1beta1
kind: Deployment
metadata:
  name: parse-server
  namespace: default
spec:
  replicas: 1
  template:
    metadata:
      labels:
        run: parse-server
    spec:
      containers:
      - name: parse-server
        image: ${DOCKER_USER}/parse-server
        env:
        - name: DATABASE_URI
          value: "mongodb://mongo-0.mongo:27017,\
            mongo-1.mongo:27017,mongo-2.mongo\
            :27017/dev?replicaSet=rs0"
        - name: APP_ID
          value: my-app-id
        - name: MASTER_KEY
          value: my-master-key
```

Testing Parse

It is important to test the deployment and this can be done by exposing it as a Kubernetes service as illustrated below:

```yaml
apiVersion: v1
kind: Service
metadata:
  name: parse-server
  namespace: default
spec:
  ports:
  - port: 1337
    protocol: TCP
    targetPort: 1337
  selector:
    run: parse-server
```

287

After testing confirms its operation, the parse then knows to receive a request from any mobile application; however, you should always remember to secure the connection with HTTPS after deploying it.

How to Perform a Rolling Update

A rolling update refers to the process of updating an application regarding its configuration or just when it is new. Updates are important as they keep applications up and running; however, it is impossible to update all features of an application all at once since the application will likely experience a downtime. Performing a rolling update is therefore important as it allows you to catch errors during the process so that you can rollback before it affects all of your users.

Rolling updates can be achieved through the use of Kubernetes Replication Controllers and the kubectl rolling-update command; however, in the latest version, i.e., Kubernetes 1.2, the Deployment object API was released in beta. Deployments function at a more advanced level as compared to Controllers and therefore are the preferred mechanism of performing rolling updates. First, let's look at how to complete a rolling update with a replication controller then later using Deployment API.

Rolling Updates with a Replication Controller

You will need a new a new Replication Controller with the updated configuration. The rolling update process synchronizes the rise of the replica count for the new Replication Controller, while lowering the number of replicas for the previous Replication Controller. This process lasts until the desired number of pods are operating with the new configuration defined in the new Replication Controller. After the process is completed, the old replication is then deleted from the system. Below is an illustration of updating a deployed application to a newer version using Replication Controller:

```
apiVersion: v1
kind: ReplicationController
metadata:
  name: k8s-deployment-demo-controller-v2
spec:
  replicas: 4
  selector:
    app: k8s-deployment-demo
    version: v0.2
  template:
    metadata:
      labels:
        app: k8s-deployment-demo
        version: v0.2
    spec:
      containers:
        - name: k8s-deployment-demo
          image: ryane/k8s-deployment-demo:0.2
          imagePullPolicy: Always
          ports:
            - containerPort: 8081
              protocol: TCP
          env:
            - name: DEMO_ENV
              value: production
```

To perform an update, kubectl rolling-update is used to stipulate that we want to update the running k8s-deployment-demo-controller-v1 Replication controller to k8-deployment-demo-controller-v2as illustrated below:

```
$ kubectl rolling-update k8s-deployment-demo-controller-v1 --updat
```

Rolling updates with a Replication

Controller faces some limitations, such that if you store your Kubernetes displays in source control, you may need to change at least two manifests to co-ordinate between releases. Additionally, the rolling update is more susceptible to network disruptions, coupled with the complexity of performing rollbacks, as it requires performing another rolling update back to another Replication Controller with an earlier configuration thereby lacking an audit trail. An easier method was developed to perform rolling updates with a deployment as discussed below:

Rolling Updates with a Deployment

Rolling updates with a deployment is quite simple, and similar rolling updates with Replication Control with a few differences are shown below:

```
apiVersion: extensions/v1beta1
kind: Deployment
metadata:
  name: k8s-deployment-demo-deployment
spec:
  replicas: 4
  selector:
    matchLabels:
      app: k8s-deployment-demo
  minReadySeconds: 10
  template:
    metadata:
      labels:
        app: k8s-deployment-demo
        version: v0.1
    spec:
      containers:
        - name: k8s-deployment-demo
          image: ryane/k8s-deployment-demo:0.1
          imagePullPolicy: Always
          ports:
            - containerPort: 8081
              protocol: TCP
          env:
            - name: DEMO_ENV
              value: staging
```

The differences are

- The selector uses match labels since the Deployment objects support set-based label requirements.

- The version label is excluded by the selector. The same deployment object supports multiple versions of the application.

The kubectl create function is used to run the deployment as illustrated below:

```
$ kubectl create -f demo-deployment-v1.yml --record
deployment "k8s-deployment-demo-deployment" created
```

This function saves the command together with the resource located in the Kubernetes API server. When using a deployment, four pods run the application to create the Deployment objects as shown below:

As mentioned earlier on, one advantage of using deployment is that the update history is always stored in Kubernetes and the kubectl rollout command can be

```
$ kubectl get pods
NAME                                                    READY    STATUS
k8s-deployment-demo-deployment-3774590724-2scro         1/1      Runnir
k8s-deployment-demo-deployment-3774590724-cdtsh         1/1      Runnir
k8s-deployment-demo-deployment-3774590724-dokm9         1/1      Runnir
k8s-deployment-demo-deployment-3774590724-m58pe         1/1      Runnir

$ kubectl get deployment
NAME                                  DESIRED   CURRENT   UP-TO-DATE
k8s-deployment-demo-deployment        4         4         4
```

used to view the update history

illustrated below:

```
$ kubectl rollout history deployment k8s-deployment-demo-deploymer
deployments "k8s-deployment-demo-deployment":
REVISION        CHANGE-CAUSE
1               kubectl create -f demo-deployment-v1.yml --record
2               kubectl apply -f demo-deployment-v2.yml --record
```

In conclusion, rolling updates is an essential feature in Kubernetes, and its efficiency is improved with each released version. The new Deployment feature in Kubernetes 1.2 provides a well-designed mechanism of managing application deployment.

Statefulness: Deploying Replicated Stateful Applications

Statefulness is essential in the case of the following application needs:

- Stable, persistent storage.

- Stable, unique network identifiers.

- Ordered, automated rolling updates.

- Ordered, graceful deletion and termination.

- Ordered, graceful deployment and scaling.

In the above set of conditions, synonymous refers to tenacity across pod (re)scheduling.

Statefulness can be used instead of using ReplicaSet to operate and provide a stable identity for each pod. StatefulSet resources are personalized to applications where instances of the application must be treated as non-fungible individuals, with each having a stable name and state. A StatefulSet ensures that those pods are rescheduled in such a way that they maintain their identity and state. Additionally, it allows one to easily and efficiently scale the number of pets up and down. Just like ReplicaSets, StatefulSet has an anticipated replica count field which determines the number of pets you want operating at a given time. StatefulSet created pods from pod templates specific to the parts of the StatefulSet; however, unlike pods developed by ReplicaSets, pods created by the StatefulSet are not identical to each other. Each pod has its own set of volumes, i.e., storage, which differentiates it from its peers. Pet pods have a foreseeable and stable identity as opposed to new pods which gets a completely random number.

Every pod created by StatefulSet is allocated a zero index, which is then utilized to acquire the pod's name and hostname and to ascribe stable storage to the pod; therefore, the names of the pods are predictable since each pod's name is retrieved from the StatefulSet's name and the original index of the instance. The pods are well organized rather than being given random names.

In some situations, unlike regular pods, Stateful pods require to be addressable by their hostname, but this is not the case with regular pods.

Attributed to this, StatefulSet needs you

to develop a corresponding governing headless service that is used to offer the actual network distinctiveness to each pod. In this service, each pod, therefore, gets its unique DNS entry; thus, its aristocracies and perhaps other clients in the network can address the pod by its hostname.

Deploying a Replicated Stateful Application

To deploy an app through StatefulSet, you will first need to create two or more separate types of objects outlined below:

- The StatefulSet itself.

- The governing service required by the StatefulSet.

- PersistentVolume for storing the data files.

The StatefulSet is programmed to develop a PersistantVolumeClaim for every pod instance which will then bind to a persistent volume; however, if your cluster does not support dynamic provisioning, you will need to manually create PersistentVolume using the requirements outlined above.

To create the PersistentVolume required to scale the StatefulSet to more than tree replicas, you will first need to develop an authentic GCE Persistent Disks like the one illustrated below:

The GCE Persistent Storage Disk is used as the fundamental storage mechanism

```
$ gcloud compute disks create --size=1GiB --zone=europe-west1-b pv-a
$ gcloud compute disks create --size=1GiB --zone=europe-west1-b pv-b
$ gcloud compute disks create --size=1GiB --zone=europe-west1-b pv-c
```

in Google's Kubernetes Engine.

The next step in deploying a replicated Stateful application is to create a governing service which is essential to provide the Stateful pods with a network identity. The governing service should contain:

- Name of the Service.

- The StatefulSet's governing

service which should be headless.

- Pods which should be allotted labels synonymous to the service, i.e., app=kubia label.

After completing this step, you can then create the StatefulSet manifest as listed below:

```
apiVersion: apps/v1beta1
kind: StatefulSet
metadata:
  name: kubia
spec:
  serviceName: kubia
  replicas: 2
  template:
    metadata:
      labels:                           1
        app: kubia                      1
    spec:
      containers:
      - name: kubia
        image: luksa/kubia-pet
        ports:
        - name: http
          containerPort: 8080
        volumeMounts:
        - name: data                    2
          mountPath: /var/data          2
  volumeClaimTemplates:
  - metadata:                           3
      name: data                        3
    spec:                               3
      resources:                        3
        requests:                       3
          storage: 1Mi                  3
      accessModes:                      3
      - ReadWriteOnce                   3
```

Later on, create the StatefulSet and a list
of pods. The final product is that the
StatefulSet will be configured to develop
two replicas and will build a single pod.
The second pod is then created after the
first pod has started operating.

Understanding Kubernetes Internals

To understand Kubernetes internals, let's first discuss the two major divisions of the Kubernetes cluster:

- The Kubernetes Control Plane

- Nodes

- Add-on Components

The Kubernetes Control Panel

The control panel is responsible for overseeing the functions of the cluster. The components of the control panel include:

- The etcd distributed persistent storage

- The Controller Manager

- The Scheduler

- The API server

The components function is in unison to store and manage the state of the cluster.

Nodes

The nodes function to run the containers
and have the following components:

- The Kubelet

- The Container Runtime (Docker,
  rkt, or others)

- The Kubernetes Service Proxy
  (kube-proxy)

Add-on Components

Apart from the nodes and control panel,
other components are required for
Kubernetes to operate effectively. This
includes:

- An Ingress controller

- The Dashboard

- The Kubernetes DNS server

- Heapster

- The Container Network Interface
  network plugin

Functioning of the Components

All the components outlined above interdepend among each other to function effectively; however, some components can carry out some operations independently without the other components. The components only communicate with the API server and not to each other directly. The only component that communicates with the etcd is the API server. Rather than the other components communicating directly with the etcd, they amend the cluster state by interacting with the API server. The system components always initiate the integration between the API server and other components. However, when using the command kubectl to retrieve system logs, the API server does not connect to the Kubelet and you will need to use kubectlattachorkubectl port-forward to connect to an operating container.

The components of the worker nodes can be distributed across multiple servers, despite components placed on the worker nodes operating on the same node. Additionally, only a single instance of a Scheduler and Controller Manager can be active at a time in spite of multiple instances of etcd and the API server being active concurrently performing their tasks in parallel.

The Control Plane components, along with the kube-proxy, run by either being deployed on the system directly or as pods. The Kubelet operates other components, such as pods, in addition to being the only components which operate as a regular system component. The Kubelet is always deployed on the master, to operate the Control Plane components as pods.

Kubernetes using etcd

Kubernetes uses etcd which is a distributed, fast, and reliable key-value store to prevent the API servers from failing and restarting due to the operating pressure experienced by storing the other components. As previously mentioned, Kubernetes is the only system component which directly communicates to etcd, thereby has a few benefits which include enhancing the optimistic locking system coupled with validation, and providing the only storage location for storing cluster state and metadata.

Function Of The Api Server

In Kubernetes, the API server is the primary component used by another system component as well as clients such as kubectl. The API server offers a CRUD (Create, Read, Update, and Delete) interface, which is important for querying and modifying the cluster state over a RESTful API in addition to storing the state in etcd. The API server is also a validation of objects to prevent clients from storing improperly constructed objects. Additionally, it also performs optimistic locking, therefore, variations in an object are never superseded by other clients in the situation of concurrent updates.

It is important to note that the API server does not perform any other task away from what is discussed above. For instance, it does not create pods when you develop a ReplicaSet resource, nor does it overlook the endpoints of a service. Additionally, the API server is not responsible for directing controllers to perform their task; rather, it allows controllers and other system components to monitor changes to deployed resources.

kubectlis an example of an API server's client tool and is essential for supporting watching resources. For instance, when deploying a pod, you don't have to continuously poll the list of pods by repeatedly executing kubectl get pods.

Rather, you may use the watchflag to be notified of each development, modification, or deletion of a pod.

The Function of Kubelet

In summary, Kubelet is in charge of every operation on a worker node. Its main task is to register the node it is operating by creating a node resource in the API server. Also, it needs to constantly oversee the API server for pods that have been scheduled to the node, and the start of the pod's container. Additionally, it continuously monitors running containers and informs the API server of their resource consumption, status, and events.

The other functionality of Kubelet is to run the container liveness probes and restarting containers following the failure of probes, in addition to terminating containers when their pod is deleted from the API server and notifies the server that the pod has been terminated.

Securing the Kubernetes API Server

Think of this situation; you have an operational Kubernetes cluster which is functioning on a non-secure port accessible to anyone in the organization. This is extremely dangerous as data in the API server is exceptionally susceptible to breaches; therefore, you have to secure the API server to maintain data integrity. To secure the API server, you must first retrieve the server and client certificates by using a token to stipulate a service account, and then you configure the API server to find a secure port and update the Kubernetes master and node configurations. Here is a detailed explanation:

Transport Security

The API server usually presents a self-signed certificate on the user's machine in this format: $USER/. kube/config. The API server's certificate is usually contained in the root certificate which, when specified, can be used in the place of the system default root certificate. The root certificate is automatically placed in $USER/. kube/config upon creating a cluster using kube-up.sh

Authentication

The authentication step is next after a TLS is confirmed. In this step, the cluster creation script or cluster admin configure the API server to operate one or more Authenticator Modules made up of key components, including Client Certificate, Password, Bootstrap Tokens, Plain Tokens and JWT Tokens. Several authentication modules can be stated after trial and error until the perfect match succeeds. However, if the request cannot be authenticated, it is

308

automatically rejected with HTTP status code 401. In the case of authentication, the user is provided with a specific username which can be used in subsequent steps. Authenticators vary widely with others providing usernames for group members, while others decline them altogether. Kubernetes uses usernames for access control decisions and in request logging.

Authorization

The next step is the authorization of an authenticated request from a specified user. The request should include the username of a requester, the requested action, and the object to be initiated by request. The request is only authorized by an available policy affirming that the user has been granted the approval to accomplish the requested action.

With Kubernetes authorization, the user is mandated to use common REST attributes to interact with existing organization-wide or cloud-provider-wide access control systems. Kubernetes is compatible with various multiple authorization modules such as ABAC mode, RBAC Mode, and Webhook mode.

Admission Control

This is a software module that functions to reject or modify user requests. These modules can access the object's contents which are being created or updated. They function on objects being created, deleted, updated or connected. It is possible to configure various admission controllers to each other through an order. Contrary to Authentication and Authorization Modules, the Admission Control Module can reject a request leading to the termination of the entire request. However, once a request has been accepted by all the admission controllers' modules, then it is validated via the conforming API object, and then written to the object store.

Securing Cluster Nodes and Networks

In addition to securing a Kubernetes API server, it is also extremely important to secure cluster nodes and networks as it is the first line of defense to limit and control users who can access the cluster and the actions they are allowed to perform. Securing cluster nodes and networks involves various dimensions which are listed below and are later discussed in detail:

- Controlling access to the Kubernetes API

- Controlling access to the Kubelet

- Controlling the capabilities of a workload or user at runtime

- Protecting cluster components from compromise

Controlling Access to the Kubernetes API

The central functionality of Kubernetes lies with the API, therefore, should be the first component to be secured. Access to the Kubernetes API can be achieved through: Using Transport Level Security (TLS) for all API traffic - It a requirement by Kubernetes that all API communication should be encrypted by default with TLS, and the majority of the installation mechanism should allow the required certificates to be developed and distributed to the cluster component.

API Authentication - The user should choose the most appropriate mechanism of authentication, such that the accessed pattern used should match those used in the cluster node. Additionally, all clients must be authenticated, including those who are part of the infrastructure like nodes, proxies, the scheduler and volume plugins.

API Authorization - Authorization happens after authentication, and every request should pass an authorization check. Broad and straightforward roles may be appropriate for smaller clusters and may be necessary to separate teams into separate namespaces when more users interact with the cluster.

Controlling access to the Kubelet

Believe it or not, Kubelets allow unauthenticated access to the API server as it exposes HTTPS endpoints, thereby providing a strong control over the node and containers. However, production clusters, when used effectively, enable Kubelet to authorize and authenticate requests thus securing cluster nodes and networks

Controlling the capabilities of a workload or user at runtime

Controlling the capabilities of a workload can secure cluster nodes by ensuring high-level authorization in Kubernetes. This can be done through:

- Limiting resource usage on a cluster

- Controlling which privileges containers run with

- Restricting network access

- Restricting cloud metadata API access

- Controlling which nodes Pods may access

313

Protecting cluster components from compromise

By protecting cluster components from compromise, you can secure cluster nodes and networks by:

- Restricting access to etcd

- Enable audit logging

- Restricting access to alpha and beta features

- Reviewing third-party integrations before enabling them

- Encrypting secrets at rest

- Receiving security alert updates and reporting vulnerabilities

Managing Pods Computational Resources

When creating pods, it is important to consider how much CPU and computer memory a pod is likely to consume, and the maximum amount it is required to consume. This ensures that a pod is only allocated the required resources by the Kubernetes cluster, in addition to determining how they will be scheduled across the cluster. When developing pods, it is possible to indicate how much CPU and memory each container requires. After the specifications have been indicated, the scheduler then decides on how to allocate each pod to a node.

Each container of a pod can specify the required resources as shown below:

- spec.containers[].resources.limits.cpu

- spec.containers[].resources.limits.memory

- spec.containers[].resources.requests.cpu

- spec.containers[].resources.requests.memory

While computational resources requests and limits can only be specified to individual containers, it is essential to indicate pod resource and request as well. A pod resource limit stipulates the amount of resource required for each container in the pod.

When a pod is created, the Kubernetes scheduler picks a node in which the pod will operate on. Each node has a maximum limit for each of the resource type, i.e., the memory and CPU. The scheduler is tasked to ensure that the amount of each requested resource of the scheduled containers should always be less than the capacity of the node. The scheduler is highly effective that it declines to place a pod on a node if the actual CPU or memory usage is extremely low and that the capacity check has failed. This is important to guard against a shortage in the resource on a node incase of an increase in resource usage later, for instance, during a period peak in the service request rate.

Running OF PODS with Resource limits

When a container of a pod is started by Kubelet, it passes the CPU and memory limits to the container runtime as a confirmatory test. In this test, if a container surpasses the set memory limit, it might be terminated. However, if it is restartable, the Kubelet will restart it, together with any form of runtime failure. In the case that a container exceeds its memory specifications, the pod will likely be evicted every time the node's available memory is exhausted. A container is not allowed to outdo its CPU limit for extended periods of time, although it will not be terminated for excessive CPU usage.

Automatic scaling of pods and cluster nodes

Pods and cluster nodes can be manually scaled, mostly in the case of expected load spikes in advance, or when the load changes gradually over a longer period, requiring manual intervention to manage a sudden, unpredictable increase in traffic or service request. Manual scaling is not efficient and it is ideal, therefore, that Kubernetes provides an automatic mechanism to monitor pods and automatically scale them up in situations of increased CPU usage attributed to an increase in traffic.

The process of autoscaling pods and

cluster nodes is divided into three main steps:

- Acquiring metrics off all the pods that are managed by the scaled resource object.

- Calculating the number of pods required to maintain the metrics at the specified target value.

- Update the replicas field of the scaled resource.

The process commences with the horizontal pod autoscaler controller, obtaining the metrics of all the pods by querying Heapster through REST calls. The Heapster should be running in the cluster for autoscaling to function once the Autoscaler obtains the metrics for the pod belonging to the system component in a question of being scaled. The Autoscaler then uses the obtained metrics to determine the number that will lower the average value of the metric across all the replicas as close as possible. This is done by adding the metric values obtained from all the pods and dividing the value by the target value set on the HorizontalPodAutoscaler resource and then rounding the value to the next larger value. The final step of autoscaling is updating the anticipated replica count field on the scaled component and then allowing the Replica-Set controller to spin up additional pods or delete the ones in excess altogether.

Extending Kubernetes Advanced Scheduling

Kubernetes has an attribute of being an advanced scheduler; therefore, it provides a variety of options to users to stipulate conditions for allocating pods to particular nodes that meet a certain condition, rather than basing it on available resources of the node. Kubernetes advanced scheduling is achieved through the master API which is a component that provides offers to read/write access to the cluster's desired and current state. The scheduler uses the master API to retrieve existing information, carry out some calculations and then update the API with new information relating to the desired state.

Kubernetes utilizes controller patterns to uphold and update the cluster state where the scheduler controller is particularly responsible for pod-scheduling decisions. The scheduler constantly monitors the Kubernetes API to find unscheduled pods and decides on which node the pods will be placed on. The decision to create a new pod by the scheduler is achieved after three stages:

- Node filtering

- Node priority calculation

- Actual scheduling operation

In the first stage, the scheduler identifies a node which is compatible with the running workload. A compatible node is identified by passing all nodes via a set of filters and eliminating those which are not compatible with the required configurations. The following filters are used:

- Volume filters

- Resource filters

- Affinity selectors

In addition to scheduling, cluster users and administrators can update the cluster state by viewing it via the Kubernetes dashboard which enables them to access the API.

Best Practices for Developing Apps

After going through much of the content in developing applications with Kubernetes, here are some of the tips for creating, deploying and running applications on Kubernetes.

Building Containers

- Keep base images small - It is an important practice to start building containers from the smallest viable image and then advancing with bigger packages as you continue with the development. Smaller base images have some advantages including it builds faster, it has less storage, it is less likely to attack surface and occupies less storage.

- Don't trust just any base image - Most people would just take a created image from DockerHub, and this is dangerous. For instance, you may be using a wrong version of the code, or the image could have a bug in it, or, even worse, it could be a malware. Always ensure that you use your base image.

Container Internals

- Always use a non-root user inside the container - A non-root user is important in the situation that someone hacks into your container and you haven't changed the user from a root. In this situation, the hacker can access the host via a simple container escape but, on changing the user to non-root, the hacker will need numerous hack attempts to gain root access.

- Ensure one process per container - It is possible to run more than one process in a container; however, it is advised to run only a single process since Kubernetes manages containers based on their health.

Deployments

- Use plenty of descriptive labels when deploying - Labels are arbitrary key-value pairs, therefore, are very powerful deployment tools.

- Use sidecars for Proxies, watchers, etc. - A group of processes may be needed to communicate with one another, but they should not run on a single container.

How to Deploy Applications That Have Pods with Persistent Dependencies

You can have applications having persistent pod dependencies using the Blue-Green Deployment mechanism. This mechanism involves operating two versions of an application concurrently, and moving production traffic between the old and new version. The Blue-Green deployment mechanism switches between two different versions of an application which support N-1 compatibility. The old and new versions of the application are used to distinguish between the two apps.

How to Handle Back-Up and Recovery of Persistent Storage In The Context Of Kubernetes

Persistent storage in Kubernetes can be handled with etcd which is a consistent and an essential key-value store since it acts as a storage location for all Kubernetes' cluster data. They ensure the correct functioning of etcd, and the following requirements are needed:

- Check out for resource starvation

- Run etcd as a cluster of odd members

- Ensure that the etcd leader timely relays heartbeats to followers to keep the followers stable

To ensure a smooth back-up, you may operate etcd with limited resources. Persistent storage problems can be eliminated by periodically backing up the cluster data which is essential in recovering the clusters in the case of losing master nodes. The Kubernetes states any critical information, i.e., secrets are contained in the snapshot file which can be encrypted to prevent unauthorized entry. Backing up Kubernetes clusters into the etcd cluster can be accomplished in two major ways: built-in snapshot and volume snapshot.

etcd clusters can be restored from snapshots which are taken and obtained from an etcd process of the major and minor version. etcd also supports the restoration of clusters with different patch versions. A restore operation is usually employed to recover the data of a failed cluster.

In the case of failure in the majority of etcd members, the etcd cluster is considered failed and therefore

Kubernetes cannot make any changes to its current state. In this case, the user can recover the etcd cluster and potentially reconfigure the Kubernetes API server to fix the issue.

How to Deploy An Application With Geographic Redundancy In Mind

Geo-Redundant applications can be deployed using Kubernetes via a linked pair of SDN-C. This is still a new concept developed in ONAP Beijing and involves using one site as an active site and the other site acting as a warm standby, which could also be used as an active site. The operator is tasked to monitor the health of the active site by establishing failures and initiating a scripted failover. They are also responsible for updating the DNS server so that the clients would direct their messaging towards the now-active site. A PROM component, which was added later on, can automatically update the DNS server and monitor health, thereby eliminating the need of having an operator. PROM relays the status of the site health and can make informed decisions.

5. Conclusion

In conclusion, while this guide offers you a good understanding of the essential components of Kubernetes, you have to carry out practical examples to gain a deeper understanding of the concepts. This guide only explains the basic functionalities, but does delve deeper into fundamental concepts. It is important to note that Kubernetes is a sophisticated resource for creating and deploying; therefore, you need to start with the basics as you go deeper into key functionalities. We hope this guide has been key in understanding the basic concepts of Kubernetes which are still a developing concept. Thank you

** How did you like the book? Could you spare some time and review it.

My Other Books available across the platforms in e-book, paperback and audible versions:

7. Blockchain Technology : Introduction to Blockchain Technology and its impact on Business Ecosystem

8. DevOps Handbook: Introduction to DevOps and its Impact on Business Ecosystem

9. Blockchain Technology and DevOps : Introduction and Impact on Business Ecosystem

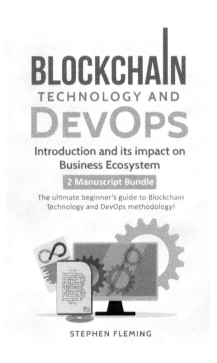

10.   Love Yourself: 21 day plan for learning "Self-Love" to cultivate self-worth ,self-belief,   self-confidence   & happiness

11. Intermittent Fasting: 7 effective techniques of Intermittent Fasting

7 EFFECTIVE TECHNIQUES OF

INTERMITTENT FASTING

Stay Healthy,Lose Weight,
Slow Down Aging Process & Live Longer!

STEPHEN FLEMING

12. Love Yourself and intermittent Fasting(Mind and Body Bundle Book)

You can check all my Books on my **Amazon's Author Page**

** If you prefer audible versions of these books, I have few free coupons, mail me at valueadd2life@gmail.com. If available, I would mail you the same.
FB: @authorsfleming

Book4: SRE Handbook

How SRE implements DevOps

BONUS TECHNOLOGY BOOKLET

Dear Friend,
I am privileged to have you onboard. You have shown faith in me and I would like to reciprocate it by offering the maximum value with an amazing booklet which contains latest technology updates on DevOps and Blockchain.

"Get Instant Access to Free Booklet and Future Updates"

- Link: http://eepurl.com/dge23r

OR

- QR Code : You can download a QR code reader app on your mobile and open the link:

Preface

Well, you have been hearing a lot about DevOps lately, wait until you meet a Site Reliability Engineer!

Google is the pioneer in the SRE movement and Ben Treynor from Google defines SRE as," "what happens when a software engineer is tasked with what used to be called operations". The ongoing struggles between Development and Ops team for software releases have been sorted out by mathematical formula for green or red-light launches!

Sounds interesting, now do you know which the organizations are using SRE: Apart from Google, you can find SRE job postings from: LinkedIn, Twitter, Uber, Oracle, Twitter and many more.

I also enquired about the average salary of a SRE in USA and all the leading sites gave similar results around $130,000 per year. Also, currently the most sought job titles in tech domain are DevOps & Site Reliability Engineer.

So do you want to know, How SRE works, what are the skill sets required, How a software engineer can transit to SRE role, How LinkedIn used SRE to smoothen the deployment process.

Here is your chance to dive into the SRE role and know what it takes to be and implement best SRE practices.

The DevOps, Continuous Delivery and SRE movements are here to stay and grow, its time you to ride the wave!

So, don't wait and take action!

1. SRE Introduction

Intro

The main function of SRE is that the system's software, hardware, and firmware will perform its tasks satisfactorily. The task being the one for which the system was designed and created. This too within a stipulated time and in a specific environment.

SRE is an engineering discipline that includes certain aspects of software engineering to tackle IT operations related issues. The main objective is the creation of ultra-scalable and extremely reliable software systems. System engineering is the parent discipline of SRE or reliability engineering. SRE emphasizes the reliability factor in the product management lifecycle. Reliability or dependability is described as the capability of a system or its components to function normally in an understated condition for a stipulated period.

The main role of a reliability engineer is to identify and manage risks involved in assets management. These risks could adversely affect business or workshop operations. This is a broad, primary role and can be divided into three smaller and more manageable roles such as loss estimation, LCAM (Life Cycle Asset Management), and risk management.

The main difference between DevOps and SRE's is DevOps' primary focus on coding and the kind of atmosphere you are in. DevOps are at the top of the pyramid in terms of software development. They are responsible for both architecture and system culture. They deliver tasks or develop infrastructure within the development process.

The Emergence of SRE (Site Reliability Engineer)

This branch of engineering has a developing importance in IT Operations. You can find more than a thousand listed on LinkedIn alone for this requirement. Although this job continues to gain importance, there is still a lot of confusion about the requirements. The SRE 2018 report has shown that the SRE role is evolving. There are many engineers who are happy in their organization but, at the same time, are struggling to explain their roles in the company. Another interesting fact highlighted in the survey was that SREs are present in all sizes of company and they hail from a range of backgrounds. It is not necessary that an ideal SRE is a generalist.

The SRE's role was first established by Google in 2003 while trying to cope up with its fast-growing production needs. Since then, several other companies have implemented SREs in their teams. Over the years the portfolio has increased with a requirement of software development and IT operational skills combined together. An SRE is expected to cover both areas of expertise.

The growth of SRE was pretty much expected, especially in the area of complex infrastructure where constant availability and speed is of paramount significance. As Google pointed out the SRE is a single point of arbiter and responsibility between Devs and Ops teams. They ensure reliable and low latency apps delivery.

SRE is a specialized job and focuses on maintainability and reliability of large environments. SREs couple operational responsibility with the competence of software engineering to navigate system architecture. They are expected to strike the right balance between development speed and reliability by using engineering solutions to resolve operational issues.

SREs and Automation

According to a reliable survey conducted recently, the most important skill an SRE must have is automation. 92% of the SREs found automation to be the top technical skill required and 18% have indicated that their teams have automated all possible aspects of the operations process. A typical aspect of an SRE is a strong desire not to see the same issue again. This is because the issue has been automized the second time around. SRE participation in problem-solving is more dynamic as they are expected to engineer away the issues rather than just restoring the system back to normalcy. If you find that mobiles and pagers are not ringing continuously on the floor, the SREs have done their job. It means that the system is more stable and reliable, and it is time to move on to another system in the company that needs SREs.

However, you need to remember that SRE is not totally about automation. The engineers require lots of both technical and non-technical skills. The survey indicates that the SRE needs the ability to solve problems, be part of a team, work under pressure, and have strong verbal and written skills. The technical skills required include logging, monitoring, automation, infrastructure configuration, observability, scripting languages and application, and network protocols.

SREs have accepted both continuous

343

deployment and cloud. About 65% of SREs are in the cloud and are deploying codes at least once daily. 47% deploy codes multiple times daily while 27% use it once a week. Another point to remember for the SREs is that it is a position for an experienced engineer and not for an entry level pro. 80% of SREs have been working for more than 6 years, have a college degree, and come with IT Operations experience. Before becoming an SRE, most engineers came from system admin, development, or DevOps background.

Reporting

SREs report mainly to the engineering and operations department. However, it can be noted that SREs report more to software engineering than IT operations. This is slightly surprising as most SREs hail from an IT operations background. 25% of SREs admitted to having more than 100 such engineers under their wings. Google, for example, has 2500 SREs throughout their company. Google is looking at them to create a reliable platform and infrastructure that allows both their indigenous infrastructure and that of their GCP clientele to be stable.

SREs work in close quarters with product development software engineers. They can either be embedded with independent product development teams or separate teams working in close relations and are looking to improve maintainability and reliability. Any company that is looking to improve their software operations will benefit from building an SRE infrastructure and hiring these engineers.

If the surveys conducted are to be believed, the work culture shift can be a hindrance. Moving the job from conventional OPS to SRE can be a difficult cultural shift, not just for the engineers but also for the departments and teams involved in the change. People are still working through the transition and are still finding that the change is far more effective than before and the presence of SREs definitely provides more effective methodology than the IT OPS. Another important factor is the availability as important service indicators, notifications and alerting solutions, as they play a significant role in the tools SREs possess.

2. Principles of SRE

1. Embracing Risk

People might start expecting Google to build a 100% reliable service. The sort of platform and service that will never fail. But the fact of the matter is that increasing reliability after a certain point is not good for the service. The simple reason is that extreme reliability comes at a cost. The stability pushes the development of new features and how fast they can be delivered to users. This again increases the cost. As a result, the team will be forced to reduce the features the maker can offer. Keeping this in mind, the SRE seeks to balance the risk of feature unavailability with rapid innovation and effective operations so that the user's overall happiness with the features, service, and product performance is increased. Unreliable systems quickly lessen the confidence of the users in the system. Remember, as a system is built the cost does not always increase linearly with reliability.

Service reliability management can be expensive as risk management is always costly. 100% reliability is probably not even a good target. Not only is it impossible to achieve, but it is also more dependability than users wish. Always match the service profile with the risk the business is ready to take. An error budget emphasizes the joint ownership between product development and SRE and aligns the incentives. It makes things easier in terms of release dates rate. It also diffuses tense discussions with stakeholders and allows teams to reach the same conclusion.

2. Service Level Objectives (SLOs)

It is not possible to manage a service accurately, let alone well, without knowing which behavior matters for the service and how to evaluate these behaviors. Due to this, we are required to define and provide a certain level of service to the users whether they are using internal API or public products. We need to use experience, understanding of user requirements, and hunch when we are defining the Service Level Objectives (SLOs). The measurements thus derived describe the basic properties of matrices which are significant. Now, what values you wish the matrices to have depend on what the expected service levels are and whether you can provide the level of service. Selection of the right matrices ultimately helps in driving in the right action in case something goes wrong. It also provides necessary confidence to the SRE team that the service is indeed good and healthy.

3. Eliminating Toil

This is one of the most important tasks to be performed by the SRE team. There is always this tendency to toil and to perform repetitive and mundane operational work providing no additional value and scaling linearly with service growth. In case all members of a team are committed to eliminating some toil every week with some quality engineering we are on the way to cleaning up the services and shift the collective efforts towards engineering for scale, development of next generation of services, and building tool chains that are cross SRE. The idea is to invent more and toil less.

4. Monitoring Distributed Systems

If you consider Google or any other empire, monitoring is an absolutely essential part of doing things right during production. In case you can't monitor a service you are at a loss and don't know what is happening. And if you are not aware of what is happening, you cannot be reliable. The SRE teams of Google are aware of the best principles and practices for building useful alerting and monitoring systems. A good alerting and monitoring system is always simple and easy to reason with.

5. Automation

Evolution of automation is a force multiplier for the SRE. However, multiplying forces does not automatically mean that the force is being applied at the right place. Doing automation mindlessly creates many problems and sometimes these problems are more than the process solves. Although it is a fact that software-based automation is better than a manual one, in most cases, it is better not to have either of the two options. A higher level system design is an autonomous system and it requires neither. In other words, the value of automation is not only in what it does but also in its wise application.

6. Release Engineering

Release engineering is not treated seriously by most companies and is an afterthought in most cases. But release engineering is critical to the overall stability of the system. Remember, most outages occur due to pushing some sort of changes or the others. It is the best way to make sure that all releases are consistent. Release engineering is a comparatively newer and faster-growing side of software engineering. It is useful in building and delivering software. Release engineers require deep knowledge of many domains, such as configuration management, development, system admin, testing, and support. Having reliable services needs you to have reliable release processes. Changes to any feature of the release procedure should be deliberate rather than unintended. SREs take care of the process from the stage of source code to its deployment. At Google, release engineering is a particular job function.

Release engineers work with the software engineers during product development and along with SREs, they decide the steps needed for the software release. Release engineers are involved in how software is stowed in source code repository to shape rules for assembling, testing, packaging and conducting of deployment.

7. Simplicity

One of the key principles of effective software engineering is simplicity. Once this quality is lost it is very difficult to recover and recapture. The simplicity of the software is a pre-requisite to the reliability of the service. We are not being lazy when every task allotted is simplified by us. Rather we will clarify what we are trying to achieve and what is the simplest way to do it. Every time there is a "NO" from the SRE to a feature they are not restricting innovation instead, they are keeping out the cluttered distractions so that the focus remains on innovation and real engineering can move forward.

3. SRE Practices

1. Being On-Call

Constantly being on call is a duty that is critical to several engineering and operations teams in order to undertake their responsibilities. It keeps the team services available and reliable. But there are many problems with organizations having on-call rotations and responsibilities which may lead to dire consequences to the service and for the team in case it's not handled in time. Google's approach to the on-call has enabled the SREs to use engineering work as the means for scaling production responsibilities and maintaining high reliability and availability. This is despite the ever-increasing complexity of the systems and their number.

2. Emergency Response

Things break in the real world. That's life. Regardless of the size of the company or the stakes involved, there is one aspect critical to the long-term health of a company. It also sets an organization apart from others. It is the emergency response and how the people involved react to an emergency. There are a few people who naturally respond well to an emergency. A proper response takes training and preparation. Establishment of training and testing processes needs the support of board and management in addition to staff attention. All these things are necessary for creating an environment in which teams can work towards ensuring processes, systems, and people respond correctly and promptly during an emergency.

3. Learning from Failure: The Postmortem Culture

SREs work with complex, large-scale and well-distributed systems. There is a constant enhancement with new features and addition of new systems. Outages and incidents are pretty much inevitable given the velocity of change and the magnitude of operations. Whenever there is an incident, SREs fix the undermining issue and the services are returned to their normal operational conditions. However, unless there is a process of learning from the outages in place, they will recur many times. If they are left unchecked, they occur in a cascading effect or increase in complexity eventually overwhelming the operator and the system itself affecting end users. For these reasons, a postmortem is an essential tool for SREs. It is a well-known concept in the tech industry. It is a written record of incidents, actions taken and the impact, root causes, and follow-up actions taken to prevent the outage from happening again.

4. Handling Overload

Avoiding overload in a process is a global load balancing policy. However, no matter how well balanced your load balancing policy is, some part of the system at some stage gets overloaded. Handling the overload conditions comfortably is a basic thing in running a reliable service. One way for handling overload is by serving degraded responses. These responses are not as accurate as the normal responses or they have less data than normal but they are easier to compute. But under extreme overload, the service cannot compute, even the degraded responses. At the point, there is no other way than having errors. However, it is critical to ensure that independent tasks are secured against the overload. Take the degraded conditions seriously. If they are ignored, many systems exhibit bad behavior.

5. Data Processing Pipelines

The periodic pipelines in a service are valuable. But if the data processing problem grows organically or is continuous, never use the periodic pipeline. Rather use the technology having characteristics similar to the Workflow. It is a fact that continuous data processing with a strong guarantee like that provided by the Workflow performs well. It also scales well on distributed cluster infrastructure and regularly produces reliable results. It is stable and a reliable system for the SRE team to maintain and manage.

6. Tracking Outages

Improving the reliability of a system is possible only if you start from a baseline and can make a progress. There are devices available to track outages. Learning from past issues systematically is necessary for effective service management. Postmortems provide details on the reports of independent outages. However, they are only a part of the answer. This is because they are written for a larger impact and the smaller issues having frequent but smaller impact and do not fall under their scope. Postmortems provide great insights for improving services but they may miss opportunities to provide similar insight in smaller individual cases. Or some other poor cost-benefit ratios. There is other information such as how many alerts did a team get during their shift, which might point to some useful information. Other similar information such as how many alerts were actionable and how many were non-actionable also provide insight into some issues. "Which services that a team is managing is producing the maximum toil?", also gives some useful information.

7. Reliable Product Launches

Internet companies such as Google can launch new products and features in great speed with rapid iterations than compared to the conventional companies. The role of SRE in the process is to make the rapid change of pace possible without compromising the site stability. Google has created a dedicated team of "Launch Coordination Engineers" for the purpose. They consult with the various engineering teams regarding the technical aspects of the software launch. They create a launch checklist with common questions about the launching and try to resolve issues. The checklist has proved to be a reliable tool for ensuring dependable launches.

4. SRE Implementation

1. Context vs. Control in SRE

One of the most important thing to focus on in SRE is providing context instead of utilizing processes that are working around control. But that is the way most SRE operates. So, what is context versus control in SRE? By context it is meant providing additional and relevant information which allows an engineer to understand the rationalism behind any request. At a higher level the context related to availability is availability of micro services and how they relate to a desired goal including the availability of dependencies. With context fixed to a certain domain, the engineering team will have the responsibility to take steps to improve availability.

On the other hand, in the control-based model an engineering team will be aware of the microservices availability target, but if they fail to achieve the target there might be some punitive action. These actions may involve their ability to push the code to production. It is always better to share context on microservices availability rather than working with teams when availability has to be improved. The challenge is to provide sufficient context to teams. Whenever a non-ideal decision is made at the operations, the first query is, did the person have enough context to make a better decision?

In a big company it is difficult to provide sufficient context so that based on the context alone the personnel can achieve the targets of their service. In these large organizations you may have to fall back on lots of processes to reach availability goals. However, there are some cases for the control-based models. Such as in case where lives are at stake such as in case if someone is writing unsafe software for the autopilot system of an airplane. It is upto the SRE team to decide how much risk they can take in selecting one factor out of control versus context-based models.

2. Building SRE Team

The teams are built to achieve certain objectives, and they could be winning games, launching a product, or implementing a vision. Irrespective of the field we choose, the result must be the same. There are some ways you can take to build a high performing SRE team, although building a team of high performers is a difficult task. The objective of building such a team is to reach a certain degree of operational excellence. You need to build a team that takes care of performance, availability, change management, monitoring, and emergency response and plan the services.

SRE was Google's answer to system admin Operations. The thought process they used for this was, as we are doing software development well, why we can't adapt the same practices to run the Operations section as well? And it turned out to be a very successful thought. Google saw both Dev and Ops teams on the same side. They understood the targets and objectives very well and as a result were able to make good decisions as the features were released. The main difference was how the company was structured. If the Devs and Ops were paid for competing goals, then they will not work together well as a team. Operations is an area of stability and the people are compensated for things such as availability and uptime. Devs on the other hand are rewarded for feature releases, which may contradict with the operations team by lowering availability.

Google was one of the first companies to realize this. Rather than placing two teams on the opposite side of the process, better results can be obtained by having them share a common goal of releasing features with reliability. DevOps and SREs are all different people assembled together for attaining a common objective. There is no fixed definition for going about things. You are required to come up with your own principles as you go along, depending on the setup.

3. Using Incident Metrics to Improve SRE at Scale

It doesn't matter whether you are looking to add a dozen users next or a million users, you are going to end up in a discussion about which areas to invest in and where to stay reliable as the services scale up. Let's look at a case study by using incident metrics to stay focused on investments. Microsoft Azure worked on the lessons that were learned while working on the service reliability ranging from startups to enterprise level to cloud scale.

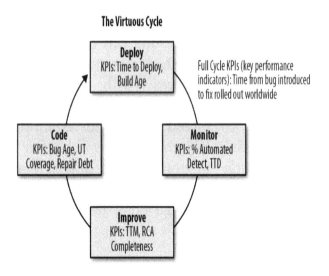

The Virtuous Cycle

Deploy
KPIs: Time to Deploy, Build Age

Full Cycle KPIs (key performance indicators): Time from bug introduced to fix rolled out worldwide

Code
KPIs: Bug Age, UT Coverage, Repair Debt

Monitor
KPIs: % Automated Detect, TTD

Improve
KPIs: TTM, RCA Completeness

a. The Virtuous Cycle

The SRE team began by looking at the data similar to any other issue resolving effort. However, when it was attempted, it turned out that there were thousands of data sources, incident management metrics, service telemetry, and deployment metrics, and so on. It made things tricky as it had to be decided which data to look at and in what order. After consulting the experts and after looking at the best available practices, the SRE team landed on a system called The Virtuous Cycle. It created a framework which allowed the SRE team to see how useful monitoring was by finding out how fast the team detected the outages. It also depended on measuring the root-cause analysis process, repairs, and how quickly the issues were getting fixed. Then the team looked at the code quality and speed of deployment to see how quickly they would run through the full cycle.

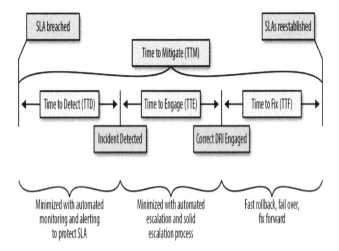

The SRE team was fully aware of how much downtime matters, so they began looking at the key metrics. They told the team how effective they were to responding to incidents and fixing them. It also meant that first, they had to define metrics that were representative of the information needed. Then agree upon definitions and timings. You could have different definitions or metrics but the group must agree on common measures and taxonomy. Agreement on taxonomy was particularly important as there might have been disconnects otherwise.

b. Metrics Review

After all these metrics were defined, the key SREs were called to look at the significant metrics that were identified as crucial to drive the virtuous cycle. Then the team tracked how they were progressing and created action plans in areas they were hitting targets. After agreeing on the metrics, the team started collecting data on how they were doing and found areas and common areas for improvement and measured the impact made by the improvements later.

The next figure shows an example of the dashboard to measure deployment and incident metrics. It allowed the team to track the trend for incident response cycle and engineer improvements in the same way as features are engineered in the product. All the incident response metrics discussed earlier show up in the figure. They measure against the targets we set and agreed on with the service owners. In case the data was found to be too much with high variability, or had too many outliers, the team applied percentile to it to normalize it enough. The outliers made it easier to understand and drive the percentile close to 100%.

	Period 1	Period 2	Period 3	Period 4	Period 5	Period 6	Trend	Goal
Σ Incidents	XX	XX	XX	XX	XX	XX.XXX%		
Σ Major Incidents	X	X	X	X	X	X		
SLO	XX.XXX%	XX.XXX%	XX.XXX%	XX.XXX%	XX.XXX%	XX.XXX%		XX.XX%
TTD @ XX%ile	XX	XX	XX	XX	XX	XX		<X min
TTE @ XX%ile	XX	XX	XX	XX	XX	XX		<XX min
TTF @ XX%ile	XX	XXX	XX	XXX	XX	XX		<XX min
TTM @ XX%ile	XX	XXX	XX	XXX	XX	XX		<XX min
% Outages autodetected	XX%	XX%	XX%	XX%	XX%	XX%		XX%
# DRIs engaged per Bridge	XX	X	XX	X	XX	XX		X
DRI Hops	X	X	X	X	X	X		X

Top Incidents	Cause	TTD (mins)	TTM (mins)	Repair Items	Impact (reported)	Impact (Actual)
Incident in North Europe due to Code Bug	Code Bug	XX	XX	1	2	XXX Accounts impacted
Network Incident due to Configuration	Config	X	XX	4	0	X,XXX Accounts impacted

Deployment	95% of clusters		100% of clusters	
	Build Age	Build Age Trend	Build Age	Build Age Trend
Service A	XX		XXX	
Service B	XX		XX	

In the SRE metrics dashboard, there are many surrogate metrics such as DRI hops, which indicate how many on-call

368

engineers are necessary to solve an incident. Auto detection gives you the figures for the incidents that are detected via monitoring. These are more actionable than the top level metrics but don't indicate success by themselves.

c. Repair Debt

A lot of insight that was derived out of the metrics review was available from post-incident review procedure. Every time a team member identifies a bug for repair it is logged. Repair items are fixed later, which prevents an outage from happening or reduces its duration. They are divided as short-term items or long-term items. The short-term items are rolled out faster within a week and they might be a script, a process, or even a hotfix. The long-term objects are more lasting fixes such as thorough code fixes, and create broader process change. The repair items are tracked in the same management system used for tracking work management. However, what is significant is that they are logged, reportable, and distinguishable in the product backlog. Repair item tracking allows us to incorporate an operational debt in the engineering procedure and treat it like feature work.

d. Real-Time Dashboards

Probably the most significant part of a metrics review is to bring the insights and metrics into real-time dashboards. If you look at the data weekly or monthly it doesn't help to drive the changes quick enough. All the services and components need to be seen and evaluated in real time where they are working, where they are performing well, and where they could improve. Dashboards have to be created which can be pivoted by a service or a manager even down to an engineer that owns the item.

Conclusion

In a nutshell, you need to measure everything, be curious, and do not be afraid to get your hands dirty and dip into the data to find the right things to do. In many cases getting these insights needed a lot of data to be hand curated but the team understood which metrics mattered and they could automate and instrument them to help bring visibility to the metrics and help services to get better.

4. SREs Working with Third Parties

No app can be completed without third parties. Most IT professionals find them a pain to deal with but lovely for their business, and they are fantastic for marketing. None of the companies know exactly how many 3rd party applications they have and what their value addition is. They are also not aware of the harm they could do to the performance, functionality, or security of the app. Developers are constantly challenged to add code and yet ensure that they don't break anything or start security holes and keep the app functional at all times.

5. From SysAdmin to SRE

The classical role of a system admin is defined generically as IT operations staff which is responsible for building, designing, and maintaining a company's computer infrastructure. The IT world is growing and changing constantly, and the role of SysAdmin is getting limited to hosting platforms and he can do it easily by applying policy around the server instance. Businesses are constantly changing these days and more and more of them are going towards Lean methodologies to achieve the efficiency they desire. The next stages of tech development mean the server administration gets tougher for manual operators and the infrastructure is delivered by a coded workflow. In such a case, you need to hire people who write the code. This is where SREs come in. These engineers know about data structures and programming languages along with algorithms. They can review the performance properly along with instrumenting and measuring it while running. Along with the software skills they have the know-how of the operational management, which ensures that the software has given capabilities throughout its operational life. These include resistance to failure, server, and site, scalability that can accommodate changing workloads and security patch management.

Several sysadmins have come into practice, having evolved from different sources such as help desk, support, or even just running computer systems at home. However, this evolutionary path will not work for the transition from sysadmin to SRE. The main reason for this is that the SRE require software skills and to understand the application itself, and you need to have learned these skills in a structured way. Learning programming at any level is a good starting point and the more you look at programming, the more you start to understand the developer's viewpoints. Several businesses in this world are on a journey of evolution and only a handful of them need SREs now. But all infrastructures will benefit from the fact that their sysadmin has software skills. All sysadmins need to follow this path.

6. DevOps vs. Site Reliability Engineering

As technology evolves, so too do the new roles in organizations and the level of expertise. There are two terms which have become buzzwords thanks mainly to Google branding, and they are Site Reliability Engineers and DevOps. The question is, do the responsibilities considered under the titles represent anything new or modern? Is there any real value to these roles or are they just buzzwords to further resumes?

There is enough contradiction about the titles as it is, and it has opened a debate on what their functions are and what is the difference among them. There are some people who take a hard look at the roles and come up with the summary that they are basically the same thing. Well, there is a lot in common, especially when you consider the undermining objectives such as automation, scaling, bridging the gap between development, and operations.

However, there is a clear difference between them.

There are dynamic companies who wish to scale at an aggressive speed who will look to lay a foundation for an IT department which is supple and agile. To do this they will need engineering departments that can create foundations for supporting the targets. The directors of these teams will need to leverage the automation tools to enable widespread conducting of infrastructure and management to several teams. There are two main branches here to perform this. One is SRE which is clearly defined to create a fully automated IT infrastructure. The DevOps, on the other hand, is more an orchestration of a Lean or Agile development team. They serve infrastructure as the code to the programmers when required.

The IT infrastructure is pretty often built piece by piece as the organization grows. The systems are built to serve company objectives from day one. Changes will be made later as they are required. Sysadmin plays a critical role in ensuring that the daily maintenance and system updates are created to protect the investments and keep a productive environment. The admins spend their day ensuring that everything is working correctly in the company. They also ensure that everything is updated and the address breaks are there when required.

There are more sophisticated IT teams which can engineer automation scripts in the infrastructure from the beginning, removing future reliance on admin. The system architect or engineer can orchestrate patches, policy, and management over the whole network via a single CMS (Centralized Management System). These systems monitor the environment proactively and detect potential anomalies within the infrastructure before they become anomalies.

SREs are more focused on the system architect's role in core infrastructure. This is more linked to the production environment. DevOps are more related to automation and simplification of development teams and their non-production environments. The major difference between an SRE and DevOps is that the focus is on coding and the kind of environment you are placed in. DevOps will always be on the creation and testing side as they are dynamic departments and use the Lean or Agile methodology to run their operations. Also, there must be automation to help manage the processes.

Developers use automation tools such as Chef or Puppet to help with the challenges. DevOps share some common factors with SRE as well. The DevOps engineer is at the top of the pyramid architecting both a system and a culture to automate the delivery of infrastructure or other work in the development process. The main theme here is that both these new roles that are SRE and DevOps are being used to help the service run more efficiently. As we move forward, we typically expect the practices to evolve and new roles will be created. What is significant is that what drives the change is operationally efficient and is fully contingent. These forms help in supporting innovation with better speed and also aid the departments to run and scale more fluidly as a whole.

7. Production Engineering at Facebook

The production engineering lifecycle at Facebook is how they build, run, and disband their great reliability focused teams along with performance, scalability, and efficiency. It was started in 2009 with a handful of engineers in a single office. Now there are several hundreds of engineers that support dozens of teams in four countries and 6 offices. When Facebook production engineers are hired they have to be good coders in at least one shell language. They need to know TCP/IP Networking, Linux Systems, Distributed systems design, and debugging, reliability engineering background and be available on call.

5. SRE Processes and Best Practices

In simple terms, SREs run services by using a set of networked systems, operated for users that might be internal and external. They are also responsible for the wellbeing of these services. Operating a service successfully means a wide range of activities, such as planning capability, monitoring, responding to incidents, making sure that the root causes for the outages are systematically addressed, etc.

SREs represent a break away from the current industry best practices for managing difficult and large services. The SRE was originally influenced by software engineering, but now SRE methodologies have become a different set of principles, practices, and a set of incentives in the field of DevOps area of expertise.

Some key SRE nest practices are:

- Support the services before they

are live via activities like developing software frameworks and platforms, system design consulting, launch reviews, and capacity planning.

- Engaging in improving the complete life cycle of services. This means from inception and design stage to deployment, operations, and refinement.

- Maintenance of services when they are live by monitoring and measuring the availability, latency, and overall health of the system.

- Practicing incident response that is sustainable and quality postmortems.

- Scaling of systems via mechanisms such as automation, and evolution of systems by pushing the necessary changes to improve speed and reliability.

The networking technology addresses

several challenges that are associated with SREs and their best practices. In order to assure optimum network performance and network operations, the SRE team needs a detailed and correct application and networking insight to ensure system performance and availability.

1. Handling Overload

Avoiding the overload condition is the target for load balancing policies. However, no matter how good your load balancing policy is, eventually some parts of the system become overloaded. Handling overload conditions gracefully is a fundamental requirement in running any reliable serving system. It is also important that individual tasks are also protected against overload conditions. For example, a backend task serving a certain traffic rate should continue to keep doing so at the same rate without any impact on the latency. This needs to continue despite how much surplus traffic is added at the task. The backend chore should not fall over and crash while placed under the load.

The statements must hold true for a definite rate of traffic which is 2X or even 10X of what the task is allotted to process. It is an accepted fact that at a certain point the system will break down and rising the point at which the breakdown occurs is very difficult to achieve.

The key to handling overload conditions is to take degradation conditions seriously. If the situations are ignored, various systems display terrible behavior. As work piles up the tasks find it hard to run and they ultimately run out of retention and crash or even might end up burning the CPU. Latency suffers pretty badly as the traffic is dropping and the tasks start competing for resources. If the condition is left unchecked a failure in a subgroup of a system can trigger multiple failures in other system components causing the entire system to fail at some point in time. The impact from this can be so damaging that it is dangerous for any scheme operating at scale to have protection against it.

It is a common misconception that the overloaded backend must turn down and halt accepting all the traffic. This conception goes against the target of robust load balancing. It is better for the backend to keep accepting as much circulation as possible but only accept the load as the memory frees up. A quality backend, if supported by strong load balancing strategies, will accept only those requests it can process gracefully and reject the others.

There are a range of tools available for implementing quality load balancing and overload protection. But they are not magic, as load balancing needs a thorough understanding of systems and the semantics of the requests. There are many techniques used by Google that have evolved and will continue to do so as the nature of systems continue to modify.

2. SRE Engagement Model Evolution

We have discussed so far what happens when the SRE is already in place and in

383

custody of a service. But very few facilities begin their lifespan enjoying SRE support. Therefore, there is a need to have a process for assessing a service, ensuring that it needs the support of an SRE, a negotiation about how to improve the negative conditions that block SRE support and really have the SREs. This process is called on boarding. In case you are in a situation where you are bounded by many services which are in a different state of completion and excellence, your SRE team is probably running through an ordered queue for onboardings for quite some time. It would have finished taking on the high-value targets by now.

This is a common and totally reasonable method of dealing with such a fait accompli situation. However, there are at least two different ways of bringing in the wisdom gathered from production and SRE care to the services new and old. In the first scenario like software engineering, the earlier an SRE team is consulted the better. It is similar to finding a bug early. The earlier it is found, the cheaper it is to repair it. The earlier an SRE team is consulted the more beneficial it will be. When SREs are engaged early in the stages of design the on boarding time is lowered and the services become more reliable. This is normally because there is no reason to unwind suboptimal design or its implementation.

The second way is perhaps the best way and it involves short-circuiting the process due to which specially fashioned systems having a lot of individual differences end up at the SRE door. Provide the PD team with a platform that is validated by the SRE infrastructure upon which the production team can build their system. The platform will benefit both reliability and scalability. This also avoids some cognitive load issues completely and by addressing the general infrastructure practices it allows the product development team to focus on innovations at application layer stage where it belongs.

It is certain that service reliability can be improved by SRE engagement. It is a process in which there are systematic reviews and improvement of the production process. The SREs initial such approach in Google was Simple Production Readiness Review that went a long way in standardizing the SRE engagement model, but it was applicable only to services that had reached the launching phase. Over a period of time, SREs extended and improved this model.

The earlier engagement model showed SRE involving in the development life cycle earlier as it improved the design for reliability. The demand for SRE expertise has grown since then and a more scalable model is envisaged. Some frameworks were developed for production services to meet this demand. Codes based on the best practices of production were standardized and encapsulated in the framework. So this meant that use of frameworks was recommended, simple, consistent way of building production enables services. Adoption of the framework has become a prominent influence on developing Google's production ready services. They were also responsible for expanding SRE contribution lowering the overheads such as service management and thereby improving baseline service quality of the company.

3. Accelerating the SREs to On-Call and More than That

The trick is to speed up the newbies and at the same time keep the senior SREs up to speed in the process. So, you have hired your set of SREs but now what? Now you need to train them on the work. You need to invest upfront in their education and technical orientation that will hopefully make them better engineers. This kind of training makes them proficient by accelerating their training process. It also makes their skills more balanced, sharp and robust.

The most successful SRE teams are built through mutual trust. In order to maintain any service consistently and universally you are required to trust fellow colleagues to know the system. Not only are they required to know the system, they must be able to diagnose system behavior and they should be available for help easily. They must also react under pressure for saving your day. so SRE education doesn't end at, "What does a newcomer needs to learn to be on-call?" Given the requirements of trust you are also needed to ask questions such as:

- How many current co-workers are assessing the readiness of a newcomer for the on-call role?

- How can we incorporate the enthusiasm and curiosity in the newbies to ensure that the existing SREs benefit from them?

- What are the activities to get the team involved to benefit everyone in terms of their education? Everyone must enjoy the process.

All students have a range of learning preferences. Learning that you will have to hire people who have a mix of these preferences. You will choose someone with one kind of style ignoring other set of expenses. There is no fixed style of education to train new SREs and there is certainly no magic formula that works for the entire SRE team. Below there are some recommended training practices that are well known at the SRE of Google? These represent a huge range of options available to make your team an expert in the SRE concepts, both now and on an ongoing basis.

Here are some recommended patterns,

- Design sequential and concrete learning material/experiences for students. Deluge students off their menial work.

- Encourage statistical thinking, reverse engineering, fundamental, and working principles. Avoid training them strictly through operational procedures, playbooks, and checklists.

- Encourage students to read the failure analysis by suggesting postmortems. Avoid efforts to bury the outages to conceal the blame.

- Create realistic breakages allowing students to fix them with real monitoring and tooling. This avoids students from having the first chance to fix when he is already on-call.

- Encourage role playing with theoretical disasters as a group to improve a team's issue solving ability. Avoid experts being created who are compartmentalized.

- Allow students to shadow on-call rotations early, thereby allowing them to compare notes with the on-caller. Avoids students from getting to the on-call situation before their knowledge is holistic.

- Pair the student with expert SREs to be able to revise on-call training plans. This stops the thinking that the incident is to be touched by experts only.

- Allow the students partial ownership by giving them nontrivial project work. This nullifies the tendency for the expert to get significant work and the newbie's left cleaning up the scraps.

4. Dealing with Interrupts

The operational load is the work when applied to complex systems must be done in order to maintain a system in a functional state. Viz. in case you own a car, someone will always service it, place gas in it, or do other maintenance work related to it to keep it performing its functionalities. All complex systems are as full of errors as its creators.

There are many forms to operational overloads when they are applied to maintaining complex systems. Some of them are more obvious than others. The terminology used may change but the operational load falls under three categories: tickets, pages, and ongoing operational activities.

Pages: They are related to production

alerts and their fallouts. Pages are triggered in response to production emergencies. They are many times recurring and monotonous, needing little thought. They may also be involving and with in-depth tactical thought. These pages have an SLO (expected response time) that is measured in minutes.

Tickets: Tickets are customer requests that ask you to take action. Like pages, tickets may be boring and simple or may need real thinking. One simple ticket may request a code review for a configuration that the team owns or a more complex ticket may entail special requests for help with a decision or capacity plans. Tickets can also have SLO, but in this case, the response time is measured in hours, days, and weeks.

Ongoing Operational Responsibilities: They are also referred to as "Kicking the can down the road" or "Toil". They involve activities such as team owned code or flag rollouts, or responses to sudden situations or time-sensitive queries from clients. Although they do not have a definite SLO these tasks may interrupt you.

There are operational overloads that can be anticipated easily or planned for but most of them are unplanned. It can interrupt someone at any non-specific time requiring the person to make a decision whether it can wait or not.

5. Recovering an SRE from Operational Overload

It is a common policy for the Google SRE team to evenly divide their time between their developments and sensitive ops work. Their balance remains upset for several months due to a surge in daily tickets volume. A massive amount of ops work is particularly dangerous as the SRE team may burn out or become handicapped to make progress on the project at hand. Whenever a team must allocate an uneven amount of time to resolve tickets at the cost of spending time on improving service, its reliability, and scalability suffer.

393

One way of relieving this burden is by temporarily transferring an additional SRE in the overloaded team. Once this person is embedded in the team, the SRE focuses on improving practices opposed to just helping the team empty the ticket queue. This SRE observes the daily routine of the team and recommends certain points to improve team practices. This adds a fresh perspective to the team performance and their routines that cannot be provided by the team itself.

However, while using this approach, it is necessary to transfer more than a single engineer. Well, two SREs does not necessarily mean better results. It may cause issues in case the team doesn't react suitably to them.

6. Communicating and Collaboration within SRE

The SRE organizational position in Google is stimulating and has a clear effect on how you communicate and collaborate. There is a huge diversity involved in SRE work and how it is done. There are service teams, infrastructure teams, and horizontal product teams. There are relationships involved with product growth teams sometimes much larger than SRE teams and sometimes the same size. Then there are situations in which the SRE team is the product development team. SRE teams are made from people who are equipped with architectural skills or system engineering skills, project management skills, software engineering skills, leadership qualities, and a background in all fields of engineering. They do not have just a single model and they have more than one configuration that work. This flexibility is suitable to their ultimate pragmatic nature.

It is also a fact that the SRE is not your command and control company. Normally they have an alliance with at least two masters, one for service and the other for infrastructure. They work in general SRE context. The relationship with service is very strong as they are held responsible for the show of those systems. However, despite that

395

relationship, the actual reporting lines are via SRE as a whole. Nowadays, the SRE spends more time supporting their independent services across the production work. But they come from shared values culture and, as a result, they have a strong homogeneous approach to the issues. It is so by design.

The facts mentioned above have steered SRE organizations in certain directions whilst taking into consideration two crucial dimensions called communication and collaboration. For communication, the apt computing metaphor will be data flow. Similar to the fact that data must flow around the production, it has to flow around SRE as well. Data could be about the condition of the services, projects, production, and the condition of the persons. For the highest efficiency of a team, service data must move in a reliable way from one point to another. One way of thinking about this flow is by thinking about the interface an SRE team must show to other teams like the APL. Like the APL a good design is critical for the effective operation, and in case the API is incorrect it will be very difficult to correct later on.

The API is also pertinent for collaboration as contract metaphor both for the SRE teams and between product development and SRE teams. They all need to progress in an environment with constant change. This collaboration looks pretty much like collaboration between any other fast-moving organization. The only difference being the mix of system engineering expertise, software engineering skills, and the wisdom gathered out of production that the SRE brings to the collaboration. A best design and best implementation happens when there is a joint concern between production and the invention being met with mutual respect. This happens to be the promise an SRE makes to an organization. They are equipped with dependability, with the similar skills as that of product development teams. This improves things a great deal. Experience indicates that just having a person in charge of consistency without the full skill set will not be enough for the job.

Considering the globally spread nature of SRE teams, effective communication will always be high priority within the SRE. The collaboration within the SRE teams has its challenges but also great rewards, including a common approach to platform for solving issues and allowing the team to focus on more difficult issues.

7. Testing for Reliability

One of the key responsibilities of SREs is to quantify the confidence in the system they are maintaining. This is achieved by SREs adapting the classical software testing techniques at scale to the systems. The confidence can be measured in terms of past reliability and forthcoming reliability. Past is captured by analyzing the data provided via monitoring the system behavior. While the future is quantified by making educated predictions from the data indicated in the past system behavior. To make sure that these predictions are correct to be of use, one of the subsequent conditions must be good:

- The website has remained totally unchanged over a period of time without any software publications or changes in servers. This means that the future behavior of the system will be the same as the past.

- You can confidently tell all changes to the website with the analysis which will follow indicate all uncertainties incurred due to the changes.

Testing is a method used to establish specific areas of similarity when there are changes. Every test that passes before and after the changes reduces the uncertainty factor for which the analysis follows. Thorough testing allows us to predict the reliability of a system with sufficient details to be pragmatically useful. The amount of testing required hinges on the reliability requirements of the system.

As the percentile of codebase covered by tests increases, you are reducing the uncertainty and increase the reliability in the system. Sufficient testing means that you are permitted to make more changes before the reliability falls below a certain acceptable level. In case you make too many changes too fast. the reliability also approaches the acceptability mark quickly. You should stop making any changes at this point while the new data accumulates. This accumulated data supplements the test coverage and validates the reliability asserted for the revised paths of execution. By assuming that the served clients are arbitrarily distributed, the sampling statistics are more reliable. They are extrapolated from the monitored metrics and the aggregate behavior indicates the use of new paths. The statistics identify certain areas that need heavier testing.

8. Software Engineering within SRE

In case you ask someone to title any Google software engineering work, they are likely to name one of the consumer-facing products such as Google Maps or Gmail. Some people may mention the underlying infrastructures such as Colossus or Bigtable. However, the truth is that there is an enormous amount of software engineering that goes on behind the scenes that the consumers never get to see and many of those yields are prepared within SRE.

Google has a production environment which by some way is one of the utmost complex ones that humanity has ever developed. SREs have readymade experience with the nitty-gritty of production. That makes them exceptionally well suited to make the suitable tools required to solve internal issues and use the cases that are related to keeping the production running. The bulk of the tools are connected to the overall objective of maintaining the uptime and keeping the latency low and assume many forms. Examples of this are monitoring, binary rollout mechanisms, or a development setting built on a dynamic server composition.

All-in-all these tools developed by SRE are developed software engineering projects and are different from unique

solutions and quick hacks. The SREs
that have developed these products have
adopted a mindset that is a product
based that considers both the internal
customers and the roadmap for future
plans.

In several ways, the huge measure of the
Google production has demanded
internal software development. This is
mainly because very few third-party
tools must be developed at the necessary
scale for Google's needs. Google's
history of successful projects in software
engineering has led many to agree to the
doles of developing straight within the
SRE. SREs are in a good position to
develop this internal software for several
reasons.

The software engineering projects in
Google SRE have grown with the
organization and, in several cases, the
lessons that were learned from the
successful execution of earlier
development projects have paved the
way for their subsequent endeavors. The
unique and hands-on experience that
SREs have brought to the development

tools leads to innovative approaches to the conventional issues. The SRE driven projects are clearly beneficial to the organization in creating a successful model for supporting the services at scale. As SREs often develop software to streamline the inefficient processes or automate common tasks. The projects mean that the SRE teams do not have to scale linearly with the size of the services they are supporting. In the end, the benefits of having the SRE devoting some of their time to software development are always reaped by the organization.

9. Load Balancing at the Front End/in the Datacenter

Google serves several million requirements every second at the front end. Obviously, they use more than just a single computer for handling all these requests. However, even if there was a single super computer that was someway able to handle all the requirements at the same time, Google will still not employ a policy that relies on a single point failure. When you are dealing with systems that are so big, placing all your eggs in a single basket is a sure recipe for disaster. Now let us consider load balancing within the datacenter. Application level policies are used for routing the requests onto individual servers which can process them.

10. Managing a Critical State

It is a reality that processes crash or need to be resumed. Hard drives also fail. Natural disasters are responsible for taking out many datacenters in a region. SREs are required to anticipate these kinds of disasters and develop strategies which will run the service despite calamities. The strategies usually means running these systems on several websites. Distributing a system geographically is relatively straightforward but it involves maintaining a consistent view of the state of the system which is indeed difficult and a nuanced undertaking. There are groups of processes which may wish to agree reliably on the following queries:

- Which is the leader of the group process?

- What is the state of processes involved in a group?

- Does the process hold lease?

- Has the message been committed successfully to the distribute queues?

- What is the given key's value in a data store?

Distributed consensus is very effective in building highly available and reliable systems that need a constant view of some state of the system. The distributed consensus means reaching an agreement amongst a collection of processes linked by an unreliable network. For example, many processes in a scattered system are needed to form a constant view of a critical configuration. This is despite whether the distributed lock is seized or the message in the queue is processed or not.

Keep in mind the kind of problems the distributed consensus can be used to solve. Also remember the kinds of problems that can arise when ad hoc methods like heartbeats are utilized instead of the distributed consensus. When you see critical shared state, leader election, or distributed locking always think of distributed consensus. Any lesser approach will be a ticking bomb waiting to explode in the system.

6. Building SRE Success Culture at LinkedIn (A Case Study)

Being an SRE (Site Reliability Engineer) means having to face a lot of tough problems. Complex failure scenarios, outages, and other technical crises are amongst the things they must be ready to deal with every working day at LinkedIn. When they are not dealing with problems they are discussing them. They perform regular postmortems and root cause analysis and they are required to dig into difficult technical difficulties in an unflinching and relentless way.

Strangely enough, discussing culture in an SRE association can be a lot harder. At LinkedIn, it is constantly discussed how the culture is equally as important as their products. And yet it is tough to have a blueprint for other teams and companies to aid them in creating the right SRE culture. One wishes there were easy steps to follow in the technology industry. Things like range and inclusion are common in the tech world. As things are, there are several companies looking to generate a positive culture but are not always sure how to go on board the process.

1. Postmortem on the SRE Culture at LinkedIn

They are certainly not claiming that they have found a formula that fit all the processes for creating the correct engineering culture. But two engineers from the team told their boss that they feel the LinkedIn culture is exclusive and as an employee they felt valued and supported despite their backgrounds.

This caused the writer to reflect on SRE organization culture specifically because he knew that things were not like that always. He has mentioned below some changes they made over the years for installing an all-inclusive culture, a positive attitude, and discussion of activities performed on a daily basis. And to maintain the procedures. Although this is not a specific guide some of the thoughts and their experiences are sure to benefit those looking to change the organizational culture.

2. Fighting Fire in the Early Years

In the earlier years of the SRE team, they were not even called SREs. Their role was more of a mixture of firefighting, release management, and conventional operations. The focus was completely on getting these things done and there was no culture to speak of. Now, the LinkedIn site was infused with many reliability issues as it was faced with hyper growth. All the tech team could think of was to keep things going. There was no time to think of the culture they were creating, technically or otherwise.

When things finally leveled up a little, they decided that they needed to make grave changes to the team to correct the various issues with the product. They reorganized themselves as an SRE team and tasked themselves with a clear goal in mind and that was to keep the website up and running all the time. In order to align with this assignment, they decided to embrace values of ownership and craftsmanship across engineering. This meant they felt totally responsible for the site like they were the owners of it. They viewed their functions as a craft, which requires execution.

This overhaul to an extent was successful. The site was moved into a more stable position and the role of the operations team to solve the issues was made via software instead of people and process.

3. Dealing with the Culture Debt

Like all the SREs, the LinkedIn team SREs are always thoughtful about things such as efficiency, resilience, automation, and the availability of team member experience. When you are tackling these issues everyday you are working with other teams or other SREs in a larger engineering organization. So we need SREs that are aware of the importance of collaboration with other people.

As the LinkedIn technical situation was terrible during their hyper growth period, they have come to value their technical skills above all in their management and hiring processes. Rather than considering whether candidates will be people that will be great teammates in the long-run, they placed more importance on their technical capabilities and how they could help in the short-term. Although, this got them some very talented individuals it also revealed certain flaws over a period. Having engineers who not exactly great team players were made the collaborative work more difficult. The work is a vital part of site reliability. In many cases it created a negative work atmosphere. After a while the experience became so painful for everyone involved that a need for change was observed. This was similar to how a technical debt builds up in a long lived code base. Over a period they made specific changes to their philosophy, people, and their processes in the SRE. This is how they solved the cultural debt that was built over time.

4. Philosophy

The head of engineering and operations at LinkedIn was David Hanke, who began promoting the SREs to have a mindset of attacking the problem and not the person involved. The SRE team's daily work is to constantly identify and correct issues and bugs. So it is vital to remember that we are all on the same team and are fighting against outages. It fostered a culture of equality and inclusion in the SRE team's mindset. So, whenever there was an outage, it was not considered as my problem, but our problem and we are all together to fix it.

5. People

In 2013 LinkedIn invested plenty of effort into formalizing and evolving their SREs interview process. Part of the process was explicitly looking for the missing collaborative spirit they wished their engineers displayed. This was of course in addition to technical abilities. Slowly this began to build their ranks with people who fit this culture as they were not just equipped technically but became a part of the culture. By the time this level of maturity was reached in the hiring process there were around 100 people in the SRE team. It was a far cry from those handful of people that started out in the earlier years. As the organization grew the ability to collaborate successfully became more tied directly to technical work. Not focusing on the quality of new hires only functioned for a while, as they were a smaller company.

6. Process

Nowadays the LinkedIn SRE team consists of hundreds of SRE engineers located in different geographic locations. To have scaling culture along with a team is challenging, but what really helps them a great deal is that their leadership is aligned towards the environment they wish to create. Everyone knows the significance of having a cooperative and all-inclusive culture and so it is their priority to preserve it. Part of it is by reinforcing the values in the daily stand up meeting.

Each day, the SRE goes along with anybody who wishes to participate in a short conference or go over website reliability issues from the past 24 hours and the immediate preventive fixes that are being implemented for every incident. As these topics are being discussed, they ensure that a solution is approached not only from a technical standpoint but from a cultural point of view. For example, if a defensive behavior is observed, they will tell the team to attack the issue and not the person. Or, in case an outage was because of a breakdown in communication, time is taken to re-emphasize that they are all on an identical team and need to see each other in the same light.

One part of these conferences is that the culture is not made a separate aspect on its own. It is always integrated in the way the problems of the day, such as recurring bugs or site outages, are discussed. As a result, you are doing your job correctly from the technical perspective and are following cultural values as well. The two are moving ahead healthily as they are intertwined.

7. Conclusion

They don't make-believe to be perfect and understand that there is still a lot of work to be done. But hearing fellow SREs say that they are treated well and with equality makes the manager feel that they are moving in the right direction. These examples, such as hiring for cultural fitting or making cultural and procedural values consistent and reinforcing these standards daily, can help create a culture you want to see in an organization.

7. SRE & DevOps: Similarities & Differences

So, how is it going? Though I have passed on useful information regarding SRE Principles, Processes, Implementation and case studies, there is one important topic I wanted to cover. There are many views and definitions on the similarities and differences of DevOps and SRE .Lets collate them and see how it shapes up!

So, while taking the SRE and DevOps names in one go, this is what the subject matter experts are saying about both of them!

1. About DevOps:

- The core reason for DevOps movement to start was the lack of production exposure of coders. They were writing codes without any idea of what the other guy in the production environment goes through.

- DevOps is more of an organizational culture which fills the gap between coder and the operation person and aligns them to the overall organizational goal.

- Overall DevOps culture is abstract class which leaves the implementation details to be customized by the author.

2. About SRE:

- SRE is what happens when a software engineer is entrusted with operations!

- SRE was developed by Google for internal consumption and overlaps with the DevOps culture and philosophy. But, the SRE is more explicit and measures and achieves reliability. Overall, SRE advice the way forward *to achieve the reliability and success in various DevOps areas*.

3. Differences

- The major difference in the problem solving approach is that DevOps team raises the problem and sends it to Dev to solve, where as the SRE team take the ownership of solving it too.

- SRE team is more confident in handling the production environment where as DevOps team doesn't interfere often with the production. Also, improving operational efficiency and performance is one of the goals of a SRE.

- SRE is an approach where the coders are given the ownership to deploy, monitor and maintain the application releases. SRE philosophy believes in taking charge and deploying developers who have operations mindset, whereas DevOps believes in bridge the dev and op gap by aligning the goals of the teams with that of the organization.

4. Is it bird, plane or Superman! Are we doing DevOps or SRE?

- According to many companies that implemented SRE in a slightly different way than Google, you don't have to decide. At Reedit, ops engineers work on reducing toil, improving deployment and scaling processes, but they are referred to as "DevOps."

- One more example can be taken of Logz.io which defined the role as DevOps and not SRE: "They fill the gap between coders and operations through automated monitoring and performance stress- testing".

5. Similarities

Both SRE and DevOps are aiming for:

- Monitor and Measure the success

- Move from Silos to collaboration between Dev & Ops Teams

- Move towards Organizational Culture more accepting of failures

- Automation

6. DevOps Pillars vs. SRE Practices

DevOps	SRE
Measure	availability, uptime, outages, toil, etc. is measured
Reduce Silos	Same tools & techniques are used by developers and ops

Accept Failure	Formula for containing & balancing failures in new releases
Automation	Minimizing manual work for long term value addition
Gradual Change	Do fail and move ahead quickly to reduce cost of failure

Conclusion

As the SRE industry has grown, there are a couple of different dynamics that have come into play. First are the consistent primary responsibilities of the SRE and the concerns over a period of time. Systems might be 1000 times faster or larger but the real need is for them to remain reliable, easy to manage in case of emergencies, and flexible. They also need to be well monitored and have their capacities planned. At the same time, normal activities undertaken by the SREs have evolved as Google services and other company products have matured. For example, once upon a time for Google a goal was to build a single dashboard for twenty machines. Now it is an automatic discovery. Just get to dashboard building and alert a fleet of thousands of machines at a time.

An SRE team must be as compact as possible. It should operate at a great degree of abstraction in the process relying on many backup systems as fail-safes along with APIs to collaborate with the systems. The SRE team must have solid knowledge of the systems and how they work. They must also know how they fail and how they must respond to these failures. This comes from working on those failures day to day.

Most practices and principles used by Google for SRE are evident across a range of industries out there. The lessons learned by established industries have inspired several other practices in use today. The significance of outages can be vital to many industries. For example, people could get injured or even die if there is an outage in the case of some industries such as medical, aviation, or nuclear. When the stakes are very high there has to be a conservative approach as the reliability is of paramount importance.

If we consider an industry such as Google, there is a constant tightrope between high reliability expected by users and the sharp focus on innovation and rapid changes. Google is unbelievably serious about reliability and they create approaches for the high rate of change. Of course, in many cases, the reliability of term reliability is also taken into consideration.

** How did you like the book? Could you spare some time and review it.

My Other Books available across the platforms in e-book, paperback and audible versions:

13. Blockchain Technology : Introduction to Blockchain Technology and its impact on Business Ecosystem

14. DevOps Handbook: Introduction to DevOps and its Impact on Business Ecosystem

DEVOPS HANDBOOK

Introduction to DevOps and its
impact on Business Ecosystem

STEPHEN FLEMING

15. Blockchain Technology and DevOps : Introduction and Impact on Business Ecosystem

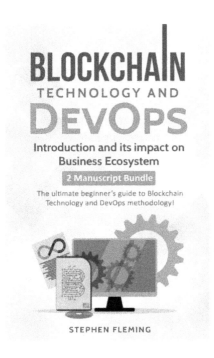

7 EFFECTIVE TECHNIQUES OF

INTERMITTENT FASTING

Stay Healthy,Lose Weight,
Slow Down Aging Process & Live Longer!

STEPHEN FLEMING

18. Love Yourself and intermittent Fasting(Mind and Body Bundle Book)

New Releases 2018

You can check all my Books on my **Amazon's Author Page**

** If you prefer audible versions of these books, I have few free coupons, mail me at valueadd2life@gmail.com.   If available, I would mail you the same.